Training Your Cocker Spaniel

Nikki Riggsbee

BARRON'S

About the Author

Nikki Riggsbee is an award-winning author of multiple books and articles for both the pet owning and dog showing public. She has shown and bred dogs for nearly thirty years and judges working, hound, and most sporting breeds in AKC dog shows. As a breeder, she guides prospective owners in their selections and educates them on how to best take care of their dogs. Each breed has special, unique characteristics evolved for the tasks they were originally bred to perform. Owners should recognize, cherish, and develop the particular talents of each breed and each individual dog. Nikki believes that taking in a dog is just like adding a new member to the family—it should be a lifetime commitment.

Cover Credits

Isabelle Francais: inside front cover; Shutterstock: front cover, back cover, and inside back cover.

All inquiries should be addressed to:
Barron's Educational Series, Inc.
250 Wireless Boulevard
Hauppauge, NY 11788
www.barronseduc.com

ISBN-13: 978-0-7641-4035-8
ISBN-10: 0-7641-4035-3

Library of Congress Catalog Card No. 2008019123

Library of Congress Cataloging-in-Publication Data
Riggsbee, Nikki.
    Training your cocker spaniel / Nikki Riggsbee.
        p. cm.
    Includes index.
    ISBN-13: 978-0-7641-4035-8
    ISBN-10: 0-7641-4035-3
    1. Cocker spaniels — Training. I. Title.

SF429.C55R54   2008
636.752'4—dc22   2008019123

Printed in China
9 8 7 6 5 4 3 2 1

Acknowledgments

The author sincerely thanks all the Cocker Spaniel owners and breeders who shared their expertise and suggestions for the benefit of this book. Among the many who contributed were Venée Gardner, Jeanne Grim DVM, Maureen Jewett, Shannon Reed, and Sandy St. John and her family. Appreciation also to Meghan Bassel, Susan Riese, Nancy Murphy, and Patricia Thurow for additional training information. I'm grateful to Elaine and Lamar Mathis and Betty and Dick Duding for sharing their love and knowledge of Cockers with me over the years. Appreciation to the people at Barron's for their suggestions and feedback, especially to editor Anne McNamara for all her patience, assistance, and cooperation.

Photo Credits

Kent Akselsen: pages 6, 19, 21, 22, 26, 32, 37, 38, 42, 43, 45, 55, 56, 59, 61, 62, 63, 64, 66, 67, 68 (top and bottom), 69, 72 (top and bottom), 78 (top), 82, 85 (bottom), 102, 103, 115, 117, 122, 125, and 128; Cheryl Ertelt: pages 47, 111, and 113; Isabelle Francais: pages 2, 7, 9, 10, 11, 12, 17, 29, 31, 35, 41, 51, 52, 54, 71, 80, 83, 86, 88, 93, 96, 97, 99, 107, and 118; Venee Gardner: pages 50, 95, 106, 120, 123, 124, 127, and 129; Daniel Johnson: pages 92 and 132; Paulette Johnson: pages 18 (left and right), 44, 48, and 105; Pets by Paulette: pages 4, 5, 15, 27, 75, 76, 78, 85 (top), 90, 101, and 131; Pet Profiles: page 109; Connie Summers/Paulette Johnson: pages 13 and 24; Shutterstock: pages 28 and 30.

Important Note

This book tells the reader how to train a Cocker Spaniel. The author and the publisher consider it important to point out that the advice given in the book is meant primarily for dogs of excellent physical health and good character.

Anyone who adopts a fully grown dog should be aware that the animal has already formed its basic impressions of human beings. There are dogs that as a result of bad experiences with humans behave in an unnatural manner or may even bite. Only people that have experience with dogs should take in such an animal.

Even well-behaved and carefully supervised dogs sometimes do damage to someone else's property or cause accidents. It is, therefore, in the owner's interest to be adequately insured against such eventualities, and we strongly urge all dog owners to purchase a liability policy that covers their dog.

Contents

1 Meet the Cocker Spaniel 1

Description 1
History 1
Temperament 4
Color 5
Points to Consider 6

2 Finding the Right Cocker Spaniel for You 8

Responsible Breeders 8
The Price of Popularity 10
How to Recognize a Reputable Breeder 11
Where to Find Reputable Breeders 13
What to Get from Your Breeder 13
Puppy or Adult 14

3 Bringing Your Cocker Home 16

Shop Smart 16
Dog-Proofing Your Home 20
The Big Arrival 21

Meet the Family 21
Off to the Veterinarian 22
Daily Routine 22
Your Breeder 22

4 Initial Training 23

What's in a Name? 23
Nature vs. Nurture 24
What to Do 25
Housetraining 25
Crate Training 27
Boundaries 27
Dinner Time 28
Lead Training 30
Car Travel 30
Handling 31
Attention 32
Release 33
Leave It 33
Patience and Self-Control 33

5 Concepts for Training Your Cocker Spaniel 34

Cocker Temperament 34
How Cockers Learn 35
Communication 36
Rewarding Your Cocker 39
Shaping Behavior 40

Timing   42
Distractions   43
Clicker Training   44
Reading Your Cocker's Behavior   45
Leader of the Pack   46
What Not to Do   48

6 Socialization   49

Initial Socialization   49
People to Meet   51
Listen Up!   51
Places to Go   52
Home Schooling: Therapy Dogs   53

7 Sound Body and Mind   55

Ears   55
Eyes   56
Skin Problems   57
Allergies   58
Skeletal Problems   58
Autoimmune Disorders   59
Phosphofructokinase Deficiency (PFK)   59
Epilepsy   60
Vaccines and Prevention   60
Heartworm   60
Parasites—Internal and External   61
Choosing Your Veterinarian   62
Exercise and Condition   63
Spaying and Neutering   64

8 *Grooming* 65

Groomers	65
Equipment	66
Training for Grooming	66
Ear Care	67
Dental Care	68
Nail Care	68
Coat Care	69
Coat Trimming	71
Show Coat	72

9 *Basic Training* 74

Equipment	74
Sit	74
Down	76
Come	76
Heel	77
Stay	78
Trainers	79
Classes	79

10 *Dealing with Problems* 81

Avoidance	81
Housetraining	82
Barking	84
Chewing	84
Jumping	85

Digging 86
Aggression 86
Resource Guarding 87
Shyness 88
Mouthing and Nipping 88
Hyperactivity 89
Separation Anxiety 89
Running Off 90

11 *Obedience* 91

Basic Training 91
Canine Good Citizen 91
Rally 92
Obedience Competition 94
Home Schooling: Tracking 98

12 *Showing Your Cocker Spaniel* 100

Dog Shows 100
Championships 100
Conformation Training 101
Conditioning 104
Handling Your Cocker 105
Dog Clubs 106

13 Agility 108

Getting Started 108
Training Obstacles 110
Teamwork 114
Practice 115
Home Schooling: Flyball 116

14 Hunt and Field 119

Hunt Tests 119
Field Trials 120
Hunting Cocker Spaniels 121
Equipment 121
Puppy Training 122
Caring for Your Dog in the Field 125
Quartering 126
Marking 127
Water Work 127
Introduction to Gunfire 128
Help with Training 129

Useful Addresses, Web Sites, and Literature 130

Index 134

1 *Meet the Cocker Spaniel*

Congratulations! If you own a Cocker Spaniel, you have one of the most versatile of all dog breeds. In a conveniently sized dog package, your Cocker is a happy, beautiful companion for children and adults, an enthusiastic comrade for hunters, and an energetic teammate in almost every dog sport or activity. While treasured mostly as a part of the family today, the Cocker has the ability to be almost everything one would want in a dog.

Description

The Cocker Spaniel is the smallest of the sporting breeds, which are dogs that assist with game bird hunting. Males are normally about 15 inches tall at the top of the shoulder and 25 to 30 pounds when mature. Females are typically an inch shorter and five pounds lighter. They are small enough to fit into an apartment or small home and easy to travel with. Though small, Cockers are not toy dogs to be coddled. They are sporting dogs with the capacity to run fields and retrieve, and they need daily exercise.

The Cocker's strong, muscular body is somewhat longer than tall. The head has a deep muzzle, a distinct stop, and rounded skull. The characteristic ears are long and low-set. The eyes are large and melting. The slightly sloping topline ends in a wagging docked tail. The tail has traditionally been docked to avoid injury in the field from rough ground cover encountered when hunting birds. Show dogs are normally docked when they are a few days old in the United States. Many countries prohibit docking today, so your Cocker may have an undocked tail. Either way, it will be wagging, testifying to his merry temperament.

A distinctive Cocker feature is his beautiful coat, which is silky and flat or slightly wavy. Coats with the correct texture are easier to care for, whereas curly or cottony coats are harder to keep clean and tidy. With a Cocker, you must commit to tending to his coat. You can do it yourself or enlist the services of a professional groomer. If you plan to show your dog or just like the look, the coat may reach nearly to the ground. Even if you prefer a shorter cut, the coat needs regular trimming as well as bathing and brushing.

History

Spaniels are called such because they are presumed to have been developed from

The Cocker's popularity is due in part to his happy temperament, beauty, and convenient size.

dogs from Spain. England and France are credited with developing the spaniels.

Spaniels were long, low hunting dogs that located and flushed game for falcons or hounds. Early versions resembled small setters, with longer tails and shorter ears.

The use of the dogs pre-dated the use of reliable and easy-to-use guns. The dogs would run back and forth across a field to locate birds. When birds were located, the dogs would crouch down to indicate the find. Hunters would release hawks into the air to keep the game birds on the ground, then throw nets over both the birds and the dogs.

Later, when more advanced guns were available, the dogs located the birds and flushed them from their cover. After the hunter shot the flying bird, the dog retrieved the game. A soft mouth was prized so that the birds wouldn't be damaged when being retrieved.

In England, different spaniels were divided by weight, size, and function. Around 1600, the dogs became specialized as either land spaniels or water spaniels. The land spaniels worked in one of two ways. The setting spaniels continued to point game to be captured by nets; these became the Setters of today. The springing spaniels would spring at birds, causing them to fly and be caught by falcons or shot.

By 1800, the land spaniels included the Field Spaniels, Springer Spaniels, Sussex Spaniels, Clumber Spaniels, and Cocker Spaniels. Different spaniels could come from the same litter. The ones with the longer legs were considered Springer or Field Spaniels. The shorter-legged littermates were called Cockers, since they were used on woodcocks.

Cockers Come to the United States

Cockers came to the United States and were eventually recognized by the American Kennel Club in 1878. The American Spaniel Club was formed in 1891. An early goal was to separate the Cocker Spaniels from the Field Spaniels, which were bigger and heavier than the Cockers. This was done by 1894, when Fields were recognized as a separate breed.

In 1920, a dog named Red Brucie changed the look of Cocker Spaniels in America. Until then, the Obo-type Cocker, long and low, and moderate of head and muzzle, with feathering on the back of the legs and underside of the body, was standard. The Red Brucie had longer legs and a more compact body. The original Red Brucie sired 38 champions.

Until 1935, Cocker Spaniels competed in AKC dog shows as one of two varieties: solid color or parti-colored. In that year, the English style of Cocker Spaniel was added as a separate variety, since the Cocker was developing as an American type different from the English type. By the 1940s the modern Cocker in the United States began to be seen as a more compact dog. Its head had a more pronounced stop, a more domed skull, and a deeper muzzle, with a sloping topline, higher set-on of tail, and heavier coat.

Mrs. Geraldine Rockefeller Dodge campaigned for the AKC to separate the English type and the American type Cocker Spaniels into two breeds. In 1946, AKC recognized the English Cocker Spaniel as a separate breed. The American Cocker Spaniel has a shorter back, is smaller, has a more domed head with a shorter and plusher muzzle, and more coat. The English Cocker Spaniel is taller, with a longer and narrower head, and narrower chest.

The Cocker Spaniel's popularity has grown over the years. It was the most popular breed in AKC registration from both 1936 to 1952 and from 1983 to 1990. Cockers have been the most popular breed for more years total than any other AKC breed.

After World War II, the American Cocker Spaniel became more desired around the world as well. The breed actually became too desirable, as many people began breeding Cockers purely for money. Dogs who should not have been bred were bred, producing dogs with problems such as nervousness and snappish dispositions and resulting in a decline in health and temperament for many Cockers.

English Cocker Spaniels are somewhat larger and with a longer head. They look different from the American Cocker Spaniel, although at one time they were the same breed.

Temperament

A large part of the charm and popularity of Cocker Spaniels is due to their temperament. They are happy, loyal dogs, and very intelligent and trainable. Well-bred Cockers are cheerful, playful, curious, athletic, and adaptable. They are very attached to their families, need lots of love and attention, and want to be with people. When isolated or bored, Cockers may be destructive, get into trouble entertaining themselves, or escape in an attempt to get to their folks. They want to be included in whatever is going on, and may push themselves in to be the center of attention.

Cockers are normally good with children and other pets. As with all dogs, Cockers must be well socialized with people of all ages, other dogs, and any animals they will be expected to meet. Puppies and children must be supervised until they have learned to play safely and appropriately together. Cockers are not extremely tolerant of rough handling, even from young children.

Your Cocker will bark a welcome to visitors, but has no guarding instincts, preferring to welcome guests as new-found friends.

Bred to hunt in the field all day, the energetic Cocker needs daily exercise and play—especially as a puppy—if you want him to be calm in the house. Most Cockers are natural retrievers, so a game of fetch can expend some of that energy. If your Cocker has a doggy friend, they can entertain each other.

Most Cockers are good eaters and love to plead for extra treats. If they don't have appropriate exercise, like the rest of us, they can get chunky.

Parti-colored Cockers have two colors. Ideally the primary color covers not more than 90 percent of the dog.

While your dog will have many typical Cocker Spaniel characteristics, he is still an individual. Some dogs are more energetic than others. Some Cockers are very social; others are less so and will want to get to know strangers better before relaxing and getting friendly. Cockers that are not well bred may have some of the temperament issues, such as fearfulness, flightiness, or lack of confidence. These can be improved with training and patience. Enjoy the unique personality that is your Cocker Spaniel.

Color

At dog shows, Cocker Spaniels compete in one of three varieties based on their coat color: black, ASCOB (see below), and parti-color, which is a combination of two colors, one of which is white.

- Black Cockers are solid black.
- ASCOB stands for "any solid color other than black." It may be cream, buff, brown, red, or silver; ranging from quite pale to very dark.
- Parti-color Cockers have a coat of two solid colors, one of which is white. The non-white color may be black or any of the other solid colors.
- Roan colored dogs are classified as partis. Roans are a fine mixture of two colored hairs. Blue roan consists of a mix of black and white; red roan is a mixture of red and white.
- All Cockers may have tan points.

Usually the different color varieties are not bred together. Since many characteristics, including temperament, are inherited, the result can be more similarities within a color family than between other varieties.

Parti-colored Cockers are thought to be a bit more playful than the solid-colored dogs. They may be somewhat more energetic, slightly better with new people and children, brighter, and therefore more likely to get into trouble. The blacks are

Children can confide their secrets to their Cocker.

from a line of show quality dogs with at least one of the parents a champion and at least half of the grandparents champions. Your breeder can help select a puppy for you that will have the greatest potential of earning a championship. Remember that while you are showing your Cocker, he cannot be neutered, and his beautiful coat must be kept long.

If you want to do obedience or agility with your Cocker, consider getting the puppy from a breeder who has earned those titles on her dogs. Puppies inherit not just the physical, but also the mental characteristics of their parents and grand-parents. These dogs need to be physically able to perform, intelligent, easily trained, and willing to please.

Similar characteristics are needed for a Cocker for hunting or participation in hunt tests and field trials. Your best bet is to obtain a puppy from a family of dogs with success in these activities. Hunting and field dogs need not only intelligence and biddability, they also need to be birdy—extremely interested in birds—and prefer-ably natural retrievers.

considered the lovers, more affectionate than others in an already affectionate breed. ASCOBs may be more aloof.

Overall, however, coat color shouldn't be a primary consideration in selecting a dog. Individual personality will have much more impact on the dog's temperament and behavior than pigment.

Points to Consider

Before shopping for your Cocker Spaniel, decide what you want to do with it.

If you want to show your Cocker and earn a championship title, get a show potential dog rather than one that is con-sidered pet quality. The dog should come

Male or Female

There isn't a big size or weight variation between male and female Cockers, but there are some differences to consider when choosing gender.

If you are going to show your Cocker, you will need to leave him intact. This means that the boys will be alert to any female in season and may wander. Intact males are more inclined to lift their legs to urinate to mark their territory. Females will come into season twice per year, with the

> **COCKER CLUE**
>
> *The smaller dog breeds live longer on average than larger breeds. Cocker Spaniels have a typical life span of twelve to fifteen years, some longer. They are considered senior at nine or ten.*

attendant discharge. She'll attract any males of any breed in the area, so you'll have to supervise her when outdoors.

If you are showing your dog, you may want to breed him in the future should he earn his championship and be of good enough conformation and quality. Whether you have a male or female determines which part of the breeding activity you are involved in. If you want to improve the quality of Cockers by producing and raising beautiful puppies, you need a female.

On the other hand, you may prefer to participate by offering your dog at stud. Breed him only to show and breeding quality females, of course, so that the puppies will be good quality. In the dog world, it is the owner of the female who decides what breeding takes place and selects the stud dog for his girl. The owners of the available males can show off their dogs at dog shows, hoping to impress the owner of a female to inquire about breeding. The stud dog owner doesn't make the overtures.

If you don't plan to show your Cocker, you can spay or neuter it. A neutered male is less likely to have prostate or testicular problems. Spayed females avoid uterine diseases and mammary cancer. Don't

neuter him, though, until he is at least a year old. Current thought is that dogs need their hormones to regulate their growth as they are maturing.

Some temperament traits differ between the sexes in almost all dogs. While breed characteristics predominate, males tend to be a bit more affectionate and needy than the females. Females are still affectionate, but less dependent. So if you want your Cocker to follow you from room to room and not let you out of his sight, get a male. If you don't want that level of affection, a female may be a better choice.

Both males and females make excellent pets, companions, and sport partners. Whichever you choose, your well-bred Cocker will be a happy and loving addition to your family.

Owning a Cocker includes a commitment to coat grooming, whether you keep the coat long or trim it short.

2 Finding the Right Cocker Spaniel for You

You've considered what you want to do with your Cocker Spaniel—show dog, companion competition, or hunting partner, or all of the above. As you look for responsible Cocker breeders, note whether each is involved in one or more of these activities. Breeders who breed just to sell puppies are not breeders you want to work with.

Remember, your Cocker Spaniel will be a companion and part of your family. That is her primary job and joy every day of her life, regardless of what other activities you and she enjoy. She is a house dog, not living in the garage, outside, or in a kennel.

Responsible Breeders

Responsible breeders are those who breed their dogs with the primary goal of improving the breed and producing correctly built and healthy dogs with sound temperaments. Their intent is to have each generation be an improvement on the previous one, and they carefully select the dogs being bred. They breed as a hobby, not to make money. They are breeding dogs for themselves and to advance their breeding programs. Your best bet is to locate a responsible breeder and get one of his puppies.

Breeders may be interested in one Cocker activity more than others. This will be reflected in their breeding programs. If you have a specific activity in mind to do with your Cocker, seek breeders who also participate in that activity with their dogs. Many characteristics are influenced by heredity. These include conformation, temperament, athleticism, and birdiness, and such attributes can help your dog excel at the activities you want to do with her.

Show Breeders

Breeders who successfully show their Cockers are the best source for a show dog. They will have all or mostly champion titled dogs in their first three generations, identified with a "Ch" in front of the dogs' names. They will come close to the require-

Reputable breeders have invested a great deal in their puppies and are selective about the homes to which the puppies go.

ments of the AKC breed standard, which describes the perfect Cocker. These puppies will be evaluated on head and body conformation, coat quality and color, and gait. Teeth and eye color are important in show dogs. Show breeders look for a happy, confident temperament with a wagging tail.

Companion-Event Breeders

If you want to train and compete in obedience, rally, agility, or tracking, look for a breeder who participates in one or more of these events. The dogs in the puppy's pedigree should have one or more obedience and/or agility titles behind their names.

Breeders who compete successfully in companion events are very interested

in biddability—the willingness of their Cockers to learn and follow instructions. A well-constructed body is always important, especially if speed is important in the sport, such as agility. Obedience includes retrieving, so dogs willing to carry things in their mouths are valued. Many activities involve jumping. A correctly built front assembly will cushion the dog's landing and result in fewer injuries.

> ### COCKER CLUE
> *Puppies from breeders in the United States usually have their tails docked within a few days of birth. Some agility competitors claim that those with undocked tails do better with weave poles. Some that hunt their Cockers say that those with tails swim better.*

Good breeders handle their puppies often (several times a day), even those as young as this one whose eyes and ears are not yet open.

Attitude is also important. When you look in his eyes, does he look back at you? You want a dog who will focus on you rather than on toys or other dogs.

Hunting Breeders

If you want to hunt with your Cocker, seek a breeder who hunts with his dogs or competes in hunt tests. He will have watched and chosen dogs with strengths to hunt well in the field. Birdiness is important, as are strong retrieving skills and soft mouths. More Cockers are competing in hunt tests, although very few compete in field events against the bigger Spaniels.

Field lines may carry less coat than Cockers bred for show. Dogs with correct texture coat, even if abundant, can be trimmed back for the field. Field dogs tend to have more intense drive to hunt.

Pet Quality

Even if you are simply looking for a companion dog, purchase a pet Cocker Spaniel from one of the reputable breeders active in the activities above. Not every puppy has a future as a show, agility, or hunting dog, and these breeders are happy to place those that don't make the cut in good homes as pets. These carefully bred dogs will have more Cocker attributes, have fewer problems, be stable in temperament, and be healthier than those purchased from less reputable sources.

The Price of Popularity

Don't get your Cocker from backyard or commercial breeders who are primarily interested in money. High-volume breeders are often called puppy mills for the numbers of puppies they turn out. Don't get any dog from an auction or at a flea market.

The attractiveness and wonderful personality of the Cocker Spaniel has made it a popular breed; the popularity went to extremes in the middle of the twentieth century. Disreputable breeders make puppies a cash crop whenever a breed becomes popular. They may sell to the general public or wholesale their puppies to resellers. They sell a puppy to anyone who has the purchase price, whether or not the home is suitable for a Cocker.

These breeders are seldom knowledgeable about Cockers, and the animals they breed are not quality breeding stock. Therefore, the puppies produced are inferior quality and have more problems.

The Cocker Spaniel as a breed is still dealing with the results and reputation produced by the earlier over-popularity of the breed. Poor breeding stock produces animals that are nervous and excitable, tending to snap. They may be shy, submissive, and afraid. Many are hard to housebreak. Some are aggressive or fear-biters. Many have health problems.

Cocker Spaniels are still popular. They rank seventeenth in AKC dog registrations, are the most popular Spaniel, and are the third most popular Sporting breed, based on 2007 statistics. As a result, they still appeal to the money-motivated breeder. Therefore, it is particularly important for you to find and select a reputable breeder to get the best dog possible as a valued member of your family.

How to Recognize a Reputable Breeder

Responsible Cocker Spaniel breeders register their dogs with AKC or the equivalent registries in other countries. They are continuously trying to improve their breeding stock and competing in events to test their dogs' quality. They are proud of their dogs and eager to tell you about the awards

Responsible breeders provide the best possible food to give their puppies a good start in life.

and titles they have won. Look at the pedigrees of the breeder's dogs. If there are few if any titles in the first two generations, seek another breeder. Don't accept "champion lines" as a substitute for titles in the first two generations.

Good breeders have much invested in their dogs and are very selective about where they place their puppies. They will ask many questions of you. They want to make sure that yours is a good and appropriate home for a Cocker and that the dog will get the physical and emotional care

> **COCKER CLUE**
> It is important that the Cockers be happy. Dogs should show, do obedience, run agility, and hunt because they want to, not because they have to.

Many breeders exhibit their own dogs at dog shows; wait until after they have shown to talk to them about their Cockers.

that she needs. A reputable breeder will take a dog back at any age, but they don't want to. They try very hard to make sure that a prospect will offer an excellent life-long home for one of their dogs or puppies. If you encounter a breeder who does not carefully interview you about why you want a Cocker and about the home you would provide, find another breeder.

Responsible breeders do appropriate health tests for the breed. They should be able to furnish you with copies of the test results when asked. Remember that all dogs are not perfect, and that tested dogs may produce dogs that don't test clear. This is a living, breathing animal that is and will be influenced by many things in addition to heredity. But the good breeders try to work with the best stock they can.

Responsible Cocker breeders belong to the American Spaniel Club (ASC). They may also belong to local Cocker Spaniel clubs, all-breed clubs, obedience clubs, and other organizations.

Visit the breeders you are considering. Ask questions. Meet their families of dogs. Puppies from these breeders will resemble the dogs they have at home, physically and mentally. The dogs should be friendly, clean, healthy, and well cared for. They should have comfortable, clean indoor quarters, preferably in the home, as well as adequate outside room for play and exercise.

Where to Find Reputable Breeders

Two of the best places to find good Cocker Spaniel breeders are through the ASC and at AKC events.

The American Spaniel Club maintains a breeder referral list of club members in good standing at *www.asc.cockerspaniel. org*. While the club doesn't guarantee the breeders, most reputable breeders belong to their breed's parent club.

AKC events are also good places to find serious breeders. An all-breed or specialty (Cockers only) conformation dog show is a competition to identify the best quality dogs to be used for breeding. While all the Cockers at the shows won't be owned by breeders, many of them are. You can ask the others who bred their dogs. AKC events are listed on AKC's Web site, *www.akc.org*.

What to Get from Your Breeder

Your breeder should provide you with much more than the dog.

A contract or sales agreement should spell out what you and your breeder have agreed to. Have this in writing in case there are questions later. Review the contract in detail, long before getting the puppy, to make sure that you understand and are comfortable with it, and to resolve any questions. Determine what provisions there are if your puppy has a serious inherited health problem.

You should get a pedigree for your puppy, which should include the names of her parents, grandparents, and great-grandparents. Many pedigrees include five generations. With each name will be abbreviations of titles the dog has earned. At a minimum, the parents' AKC registration numbers should be listed. The color(s) of each dog should also be noted.

You should also receive a medical record that includes information that you can give to your veterinarian. It should list the dates and medical data about worming and inoculations, medications, and heartworm preventative your puppy has had. It may include the results of health tests given to the puppy or her parents.

Ask for information on the type of food your puppy is eating, the amounts, and the times fed. Maintain the same diet at least for the short term, to avoid tummy upsets. Get your breeder's recommendations on future foods as well.

Get a towel from your breeder—one that has been among the bedding with the puppy's dam and littermates. This will bring the smell of her first home with her, and comfort your Cocker during the transition. Remember that a dog's sense of smell is hugely more developed than yours and important to your dog's understanding of the world.

Get a list of instructions. Hopefully it will be written, although you may have to take notes on the information your breeder dispenses. It may include crate and bedding suggestions, grooming tools, products, and methods, and training she has already had. Your breeder will be your resource for the life of your puppy. A list of Do's and Don'ts gives you a head start.

Registration Certificate

Your breeder should supply either your Cocker's registration certificate or an application for the registration papers. In the United States, these should be for AKC registration. In other countries, papers should come from comparable registries.

If the puppies are not AKC-registered, find another breeder. AKC is the oldest and the only not-for-profit registry in the United States. It inspects breeders who produce more than a minimum number of litters and puppies. If breeders cannot pass inspections or don't abide by AKC rules, they can be suspended.

Many backyard and commercial breeders don't want to comply with AKC's minimum requirements. So they invent their own "registries." They may have letters to resemble or sound like AKC, but they aren't. They may provide a form or certificate that looks official, but it isn't worth anything.

Types of Registration

The AKC provides two types of registration: full or limited. Which is issued is determined by the breeder based on an evaluation of each puppy. If the puppy is intended to be shown and possibly bred, it is given full registration. If the puppy will not be shown or bred, it may get limited registration.

Dogs with either registration can participate in most AKC activities, but only those with full registration can compete for and earn their conformation championships. This is because dog shows are intended to identify breeding animals. If a dog with limited registration is bred, its offspring are not eligible for AKC registration.

Puppy or Adult

Many folks automatically plan to get a puppy. There are many reasons to do so.

COCKER CLUE

It usually takes a month for an adult dog to become completely integrated into your family. She has memories and a history. She has no idea why she is now in your home, what to expect, how to behave, why she isn't where she used to be. Give her time to acclimate to her new environment.

For starters, you will have her longer and you can train her your way and hopefully avoid problems. Plus, Cocker puppies are adorably cute and appealing.

On the other hand, puppies need to be housebroken, socialized, and civilized. They are more active than adults. They need to learn not to put their mouths and teeth on everything: furniture, plants, cords, the cat, the children, and you. Puppies are a lot of work.

There are advantages to adult dogs. You'll know exactly what you are getting, both mentally and physically, and you'll be aware of existing habits. (Puppies aren't really a blank slate; they have their own personalities that will evolve over time.) Most adults have had some training, so you won't be starting from the beginning. Adults tend to be housebroken and have finished teething. They also have lower energy levels than puppies, even in an active breed like Cockers.

Responsible breeders often have older puppies and adult Cockers. These may be retired show dogs or dogs that didn't turn out quite as planned. Good breeders will take their dogs back at any age; they may have a dog that was returned by an owner who could no longer care for the animal. These older dogs can make fine pets.

Rescue groups are another source for adult Cockers. "Rescue" is the term used to identify the activity and people involved in helping dogs find new homes. Cockers end up in a rescue for any number of reasons. The owners could have had health or economic problems, or the puppy might have been purchased on impulse and turned out to be more of a commitment than the owners could handle. The owners may not have adequately trained or exercised the dog, and then become impatient with her. Cocker grooming may have been a bigger job than the owners were willing to do. If you are willing and able, with a little effort, time, and patience, one of these Cockers may be just right for you.

3 *Bringing Your Cocker Home*

Shop Smart

Before your Cocker comes home, stock up on the supplies that he will need. Use common sense and ask for suggestions from your breeder. There is much to get before your puppy arrives.

Collars

Your Cocker will change collar sizes as he grows, so don't invest in expensive puppy collars. Look for lightweight and soft styles, such as quick-clip nylon and buckle collars that adjust in length as the puppy grows. Some owners prefer rolled leather collars, as these are less abrasive on the coat and cause less matting. Check the collar size at least weekly so you can lengthen it or purchase a new one when necessary. The collar should fit snugly, but you should always be able to easily slip one or two fingers under it. Affix a tag with your phone number to the collar.

Many owners don't keep a collar on their Cocker in the house. If you choose to do the same, make certain that your dog cannot escape the house. Having your Cocker microchipped can help to reunite you, should he escape. Some breeders microchip their Cockers before placing them in their new homes.

Different types of collars are used for different activities. In puppy kindergarten and beginning obedience classes, buckle or quick-clip collars are preferred. Slip collars that include a slide mechanism that allows the collar to quickly be made lighter or looser may also be recommended. Other obedience classes recommend slip or choke collars made of nylon or metal.

Dogs in agility are usually collarless during the competition, although flat buckle or rolled leather collars without tags are permitted.

For dog shows, martingale (a type of slip collar) or slip leads are typically used. They are kept high on the Cocker's neck to show its length.

Harnesses, which fit over the dog's shoulders rather than the neck, can rub, especially under the front legs, causing the coat to mat. They also encourage pulling, since the dog is pushing against the harness, and there is no uncomfortable pressure on his neck. They are, however, the preferred equipment for tracking trials, where the dog does pull on the trail.

Leads

Leads come in a variety of lengths and material. Nylon is probably the sturdiest—it can get wet and is less tempting to chew

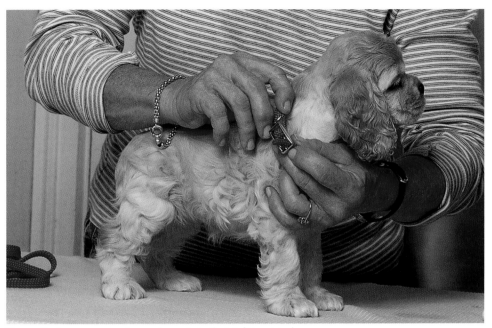

If your Cocker wears a collar, make certain that it fits properly.

than leather. A six-foot lead is ideal for neighborhood walks and obedience training. Long lines in 12- and 18-foot lengths are used for early training of activities where your Cocker will eventually be off lead, such as agility and hunting. They are also used for tracking, to give the dog a wider area to explore.

Flexible leads have gained popularity. They extend and then automatically retract back into a hand-held case. While these styles provide a longer lead without risk of tangling, they are harder to hold than traditional leashes. If dropped, the plastic case bounces behind your Cocker, usually causing him to run off in fear of the "monster" chasing on his heels.

Toys

Toys add joy to life, providing entertainment and exercise. Your playful Cocker will be thrilled with items that squeak, squeal, and move or those that can be tossed and returned, providing both fun and a workout. Make sure that the toy has no pieces that can be easily chewed off, and that the toy itself is not small enough to be swallowed.

Some toys are meant for chewing. These provide your puppy with an alternative to sharpening his teeth on the furniture, shoes, and other items. Supervise so that he doesn't chew off pieces small enough to be swallowed or choked on.

Cocker toys can stimulate and educate.

Your Cocker's bed should be a place where he can get away for awhile to rest and relax.

COCKER CLUE
Invented Toys

Cockers may get bored with old toys and are excited by new ones. Use your imagination to provide creative playthings. A carrot is a tasty chew toy; an orange makes a flavored ball. Plastic bottles bounce in odd directions and are fun to chase. Ice cubes skitter across the floor, are interestingly cold, and are good to crunch. Empty boxes and tubes from paper products and wrapping paper all make great toys for a curious Cocker. Just don't give your puppy old shoes or socks to play with; he won't know the difference between those he's allowed to chew on and those he's not.

Bones for chewing should be those intended for that purpose, not those from your leftover meals, which can splinter and harm your dog. Sterilized bones are a good choice. Unlike rawhide, pigs' ears, hooves, and the like, your puppy cannot chew off a fragment and eat it.

A Place of His Own

Everyone needs a place to get away from it all to rest and sleep undisturbed. There are many styles of beds to choose from for your Cocker, from mats of different sizes and thicknesses to beds that resemble furniture. Have several, but get those that can be easily cleaned.

Dogs are den animals and will pick out a corner or a space under a table for their special place. You can provide such a place with a dog crate. Most new dog owners worry that their pet will consider the crate a jail cell, but your dog doesn't. It is his safe haven. Make it a pleasant refuge, with a soft bed, plenty of toys, and chewies.

Get a crate sized for an adult Cocker. You can choose from metal styles in which the puppy can see out from all four sides and the top or plastic versions, also called airline kennels, with metal doors and holes for visibility on the sides and back.

Snoods come in many attractive fabrics.

Grooming Supplies

Begin grooming your Cocker shortly after your bring him home. Your breeder can suggest combs and brushes, shampoos and rinses, and possibly tools for nail and coat trimming. If you are going to be doing your own grooming or if you plan on showing your Cocker, you may want to invest in a grooming table. This puts the dog at a suitable height for you to work with him. See Chapter 8 on *Grooming* for more on products and tools. What to purchase will depend on how much grooming you do yourself and how much you use a professional groomer.

Clothes Make the Cocker

If you live in a colder climate and keep your Cocker in a short haircut, consider getting a doggy sweater as protection from the cold during the winter months. Durable booties are available for dogs dealing with ice and snow. At a minimum the wrap should cover the dog's body. Those that cover the neck and legs are even better. Dogs most susceptible to the cold are puppies and senior citizens, the sick and the frail.

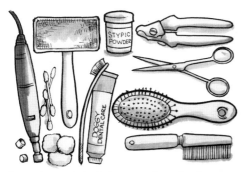

Grooming tools include a metal comb, pin brush, scissors, nail clipper, styptic powder, slicker brush, and dental and ear cleaning products.

A snood, a fabric tube that fits over a dog's skull and holds the ears close to the head, will keep your Cocker's long ears out of his food and water bowls.

Time to Eat

Your Cocker will need bowls for food and water. Stainless steel types are unbreakable, unchewable, and easy to clean. Deep, narrow bowls help keep the ears and coat out of the food and water. You'll want to continue to use the same food as the breeder, at least for awhile. Your breeder may even send some food home with you and your puppy.

Dog-Proofing Your Home

Your Cocker Spaniel should not have access to your entire home right away—especially if he is not housetrained. Limit his access to one or two rooms initially, and make these the areas where the family spends much of its time—your Cocker wants to be with you. There should also be easy access to the door so you can get him outside quickly to potty.

Limit your puppy's access by various means. His crate is a safe place when you cannot keep an eye on him. Baby gates can keep him in or out of a room. Exercise pens, portable fences with hinged panels designed to contain a dog in a larger area, are also useful. These have no floor to protect from accidents, so you'll need to put down newspaper (for a non-porous floor) or tarp or a remnant of vinyl (to protect carpeting). Many Cocker people get puppy playpens, which are larger than individual crates and have floors for easy clean-up.

Thoroughly check out the place your puppy will be quartered, and pick up or put away anything that might be dangerous to him. Remove small items that might be eaten and get cords and wires out of the way. Cleaning supplies, batteries, antifreeze, oil, and pesticides—including flea and tick products—must be shut away. Perfumes, aftershaves, potpourri, and medicines must also be out of reach. Keep poisonous plants off the floor and away from the dog. Make sure garbage and wastebaskets are not accessible.

A Safe Yard to Play In

The first element of a safe yard is a fence. Most dog owners use an aboveground fence, at least four feet tall, either chain link or privacy. Make certain that there are no gaps in the fence where a puppy might squeeze through. You may also consider an underground electric fence, with which your dog must wear a special collar. When the dog gets near the fence's underground wire, the collar will give him a mild electric shock. An electric fence may not deter a dog in hot pursuit of prey, if the dog is willing to take the mild shock. Then, once outside the yard, the fence may deter the dog from returning.

COCKER CLUE
Many plants can be hazardous to your Cocker's health, including daffodils, lilies, and tulips. For safety, don't give your puppy access to any plant—inside or out.

Fences can keep your Cocker in or away from something for his own safety.

Don't leave your Cocker outside in your yard for extended periods without supervision. He wants to be with you. Alone, he is likely to be bored and will find ways to entertain himself, most likely by barking, digging, or both.

The Big Arrival

Your Cocker is finally home. This is an exciting time for you and a huge change for your puppy—the biggest in his whole life—and he has no idea what is going on. Make it as easy and uneventful as possible from his perspective. If possible, have someone home full-time for a few days until he is settled.

Take him to the place you want him to use to potty. Let him sniff and wander around. When he goes, pet him, and tell him calmly what a good boy he is.

Show him the water bowl and let him explore his new surroundings at his own pace. Some Cockers are very curious and brave, while others need to build their confidence and explore more slowly.

Show him the crate that will double as his bed. Make sure to toss in a few small toys and a chew bone. Most important, include the towel from the breeder, with the wonderful smells of his mother and littermates. It will be reassuring to your Cocker.

Meet the Family

Have family members meet your new Cocker one at a time. The puppy may be more comfortable if people, especially children, sit on the floor. While they can hold the puppy on their laps, don't let children carry him. Cockers aren't fragile, delicate pets or stuffed toys. They are sporting dogs and can walk on their own just fine.

Don't overwhelm the puppy. Let him make the advances and decide whom he wants to meet. Supervise him with children. Some children are too fast or too loud for a sensitive Cocker, who may become frightened or defensive and snap.

Introduce your Cocker to other pets slowly, one at a time, with close supervision. Keep larger dogs under control. Pet the current dog, make him feel special, so that he will be more likely to welcome the new puppy and not be jealous. Continue this unequal treatment in the following days and weeks, feeding your current dog first, petting him first, let him go through a door first, all to reinforce his senior rank. Make sure they are comfortable with each other in the house before letting them in the yard together. The puppy will look to

the older dog for guidance, and your current pet will help you train the puppy.

Cats shouldn't be a danger to your puppy, but introduce them slowly. The cats will get accustomed to the newcomer's scent gradually. Cats generally don't welcome new pets as quickly as dogs.

Watch your Cocker with birds. They are bird dogs, after all. If you have birds, always supervise when your Cocker is near.

Off to the Veterinarian

Before your puppy arrives, make an appointment with your veterinarian. This check-up will verify that the puppy is as healthy and fit as the breeder represented. Bring the health record from the breeder. Your veterinarian will review your Cocker's vaccination schedule and advise you on the remaining inoculations. If it has not already been done, have your puppy microchipped.

The microchip is the size of a grain of rice and is inserted between a dog's shoulder blades. Have the chip number recorded in a national registry so that your dog can be identified and returned to you if he ever runs off or gets lost.

Daily Routine

Dogs like regular routines and schedules, which give them a feeling of security and reliability. You are responsible for establishing the routines your Cocker needs. The more constant you are in following the schedule, the more progress your puppy will make in learning the house rules. This includes feeding schedules, potty breaks, playtime, and walks.

Don't allow your puppy to do anything you don't want your adult Cocker to do. If your adult Cocker won't be sleeping on your bed, don't invite your puppy up to join you for a cuddle. If you don't want an adult Cocker on the furniture, don't allow your puppy on the couch.

Your Breeder

Keep in touch with your breeder and share photographs with her. She will appreciate hearing from you and learning about how your Cocker is doing. You can also rely on her. She is your resource for advice and information about caring for your growing puppy. As your puppy matures, the contact may be less frequent, but do send regular "puppy updates" to let her know how things are going.

4 *Initial Training*

Your puppy begins learning from the day she is born. Early lessons involve discoveries about herself, her family, and her immediate environment, and how they all function. The lessons you provide will teach her to become a well-behaved, welcome member of the family. You will let her know which behaviors are desired and which are not, and teach her the rules of the household. Your early investment will pay dividends for your dog's life and the life and time you two share.

Dogs are learning all the time, so don't wait to begin. Consider your puppy's age, and make the lessons age appropriate. Make training happy, fun experiences for both of you. Lessons should be frequent, but brief. Puppies have very short attention spans.

What's in a Name?

Your Cocker will have her official AKC registered name on her registration certificate. What you choose to call her may or may not be connected to her registered name.

A two-syllable call name is usually best since it can most easily be called out. One syllable can be too short when calling the dog, and often gets expanded to two syllables anyway. (As in, "Bi – ill, Come!") More than two syllables can be too long to shout along with commands.

Crisp consonant and distinct vowel sounds, such as Timber or Lady, are good. Some names, such as Lylith, are harder to say quickly with a punch. The name shouldn't rhyme with any other word you expect your puppy to learn. "Beau" sounds like "No!" "Kit" sounds like "Sit." To avoid confusion, don't choose the name of someone else in the family or a friend who often visits.

Dogs are sensitive to how people behave, so don't pick a name that elicits a negative reaction. Naming a dog "Killer" may make a person more nervous when meeting the dog, and the dog will pick up on the person's anxiety. A dog named "Rowdy" might live up to his name. Conversely, a proud or popular name produces good reactions from people, and your Cocker will pick up on that, too.

Many people wait a day or two to see if a dog's personality suggests a name. Remember, though, that your Cocker is a baby, and her behavior will change as she matures. "Puddles" or "Baby" may not suit her adult personality.

What your Cocker can become is almost entirely up to you. Always try to be the best owner that you can.

Nature vs. Nurture

There is an ongoing argument about which has more influence on a being: nature, that which is inherited from parents, or nurture, the care received, interaction with the environment, and actual experiences. Both have a great deal of influence on the dog your Cocker puppy is and will become. Temperament and personality tendencies as well as physical characteristics are inherited.

Well-bred Cockers will approximate a typical Cocker temperament: gentle, loving, playful, eager to be with their people, friendly, curious, and always ready for fun and games. That is one big reason to seek out a responsible breeder. But even within the range of well-bred dogs, there will definitely be individual differences the puppies are born with.

Nurture, the environment in which the puppy is raised and what she is taught, can have an enormous impact on the dog your Cocker becomes. Some of this is begun by the breeder. It includes handling the puppies every day, acquainting them with various noises, smells, and surfaces, introducing them to various people and animals, learning to be groomed, learning to be a dog, and more.

You, her owner, need to continue the process by continuing her education and by exposing her to numerous positive experiences with other people, animals, and places so that she will be all that she can be.

What to Do

You will be teaching your puppy what is and isn't acceptable. Make it fun, and your Cocker will learn faster. Reward her when she does what you want. The reward can be food, petting, toys, verbal praise, or getting to do something she wants, such as playing a game or going out through a door.

The best strategy for handling problems is avoidance. In other words keep your Cocker from getting into trouble in the first place. For the first year or so, your puppy will be trying and exploring many activities, to see what works and what is fun. If you can prevent her from doing things you don't want, she won't form the habit and will be unlikely to do them when she is mature.

Remember, it is your job to be in control. Don't let her do anything you don't want her to do. If she chewed the couch, it is because you allowed her to get to it and have unsupervised time to chew. If she got into the garbage, it is because it was available to her.

Keep her confined and supervised, earning freedom little by little as she can handle the responsibility. Crates, exercise pens, and baby gates can keep your puppy confined and away from potential trouble spots.

Housetraining

Housetraining—teaching your Cocker to evacuate in the place of your choosing—is mostly a matter of control and consistency. Investing the effort immediately should get you a reliably housetrained puppy by

COCKER CLUE	
How Often Does a Puppy Need to Go?	
7–10 weeks	once an hour
10–13 weeks	every 1–3 hours
13–18 weeks	every 3–4 hours
19+ weeks	every 5–6 hours

the time she is five to six months of age. Start from the day she comes home to avoid as many accidents and bad habits as possible.

Limit your puppy's access in the house and watch her closely when she has choices. The crate is your best tool. Dogs don't want to soil their beds. They will fuss and make a noise to get out of the crate when they have to go. This is your cue to get your Cocker outside immediately. Remember that puppies don't have much holding power; you have only a few seconds, maybe a minute. The younger and less trained your puppy is, the more she should be confined to her crate when someone cannot monitor her behavior.

When she is outside of her crate, confine her to a limited space with pens and baby gates so you can easily monitor her. She will give a few seconds warning before she has to go. That is your signal to whoosh her outside to "the place."

Creatures of Habit

Dogs are creatures of habit, and you can capitalize on this trait by using a schedule. Feed meals at precise times every day. During housetraining schedule water too, providing it at five specific times each day rather than having it always available.

An alternative to a crate, this puppy playpen is big enough to accommodate two Cockers.

What goes in on time comes out on time. Don't feed or offer water within three hours of bedtime. If you can get your Cocker's system on a schedule, you will better anticipate when she has to go.

When limiting her water to specific times during housetraining, make sure that she gets enough. She needs one cup of water each day for each ten pounds of body weight, more on warm days and during and after exercise.

She needs to go when she wakes up, even from a nap. This may also mean that she will have to go in the middle of the night for awhile. She may need to go after eating and in the middle of playing. When she does go, praise her calmly. Consider connecting a word to the behavior to get her to eliminate on command. Consider picking a word like "Busy!" You and she will know what you mean, but you won't be advertising your intent to others within earshot.

Part of the "creature of habit" behavior is your dog wanting to use the place to potty that she used before; she knows that place by smell. If she has an accident, pick it up (or soak it up), and take it to the place you want her to go, so that place will have the smell. Then clean the spot in which the accident occurred to remove the odor. White vinegar is effective at removing urine smells. Don't use ammonia products, since urine contains ammonia. A small wet-dry vacuum makes cleaning carpets much easier.

Take your Cocker out to potty often. An "empty" dog is less likely to have acci-

Get a crate big enough to allow an adult Cocker to comfortably stand up, turn around, and lie down.

dents. Males often have to urinate two or more times to be relatively empty, since they push the urine out. Females relax the muscles, and the urine just flows out. When outside or taking a walk to potty, don't always go back inside or end the walk when the pottying is done. Your puppy may see that as punishment—the outside or walk time ends after she goes—and she may postpone going to prolong being outside.

When you go on a walk, take plastic bags with you. When your Cocker defecates away from home, bag the stool, and take it home to dispose of. Your neighbors will be happier if you are a responsible dog owner.

Crate Training

The crate is your Cocker's home within a home. If you don't acclimate her to it as a youngster, though, it will be harder to do so later. She should think of the crate as her bed and her refuge. You can use it as an aid to housetraining. It also is a method of teaching her to deal with "alone" time.

You can have one crate or more than one. A crate in the family living area near the door to go out is great during the day. Your Cocker will want to be near the family, even when crated. A crate in the bedroom works well at night, as it will allow you to hear her ask to go out.

The crate should be a pleasant place for your Cocker, not a jail or punishment.

Outfit it with a soft, cushy bed and toys to squeak and chew. Many owners even feed their puppies in the crate.

Boundaries

Boundaries include both territorial and behavioral limits. Dogs need to know what they are and are not allowed to do. It is up to you to provide rules and be consistent in enforcing them. All in the family must participate. If one doesn't feed the puppy from the dinner table, but another does, you will have a Cocker who begs for food.

Your fenced yard provides a boundary outside. Outside your yard, your Cocker will be on lead. Inside your home, crates, pens, and baby gates limit the space she is allowed in. As she matures and behaves

27

Fences can limit your Cocker's territory while she is learning the house rules.

a high water content. They are also messier to eat and may get into your Cocker's coat. Moist foods aren't good for a regular diet because they are high in sugar and use dyes which may affect your dog's coat color. Kibble is the most commonly used, and is usually the healthiest, and most economical choice.

In choosing a food, select among the premium brands that have established reputations for consistent high quality. Foods are formulated for different ages and activity levels. Puppy food is more concentrated, to give your puppy the nutrients needed in the smaller amounts he can eat. At six months to a year, gradually convert to adult food.

Table scraps are not recommended. They upset your puppy's diet, undoing all the good work of the dog food companies to provide carefully balanced ratios of proteins, fats, carbohydrates, and so on. They also increase calories, which can contribute to obesity, a common problem with food-loving Cockers.

While it is possible to free-feed your Cocker, there are benefits to feeding specific amounts at certain times. That is especially important if you have more than one pet, for you need to know who is eating how much. A good routine is to feed your Cocker at defined times, in her crate. You will know how much she is eating, and whether she is off her food and possibly sick. Scheduled feeding is a big help in housetraining, too.

The long, beautiful Cocker ears can get in the way or get soiled when your dog eats. A snood, described in Chapter 3, can keep her ears up and out of the way and out of her meal.

responsibly, little by little you can give her more access in the house. But it is up to you which rooms she can go in. Just don't shut her away from her family, or you will have a very unhappy puppy.

Dinner Time

If your breeder didn't provide a recommendation, you can consult your veterinarian about quality foods. Dog foods come in an amazing and confusing variety. Commercial foods are available in canned, moist, and dry kibble. Canned foods have

Having your child help with feeding your
Cocker will teach the child responsibility, while
the dog will gain respect for the child as the
food provider.

Treats

Cockers are usually easy keepers; they tend
to eat their food eagerly and are seldom
picky eaters. As a result, many Cockers are
too fat. Dogs love treats. You will use
treats for training, to reward good behavior, and just for fun. But watch the
amount. Too many and you'll have a
chunky Cocker—not good for a long and
healthy life. If you give lots of treats,
reduce her meal amounts so that she gets
only the calories that she needs.

Consider some low-calorie treats. Some
dogs like ice cubes; most enjoy carrots.
You can also break dog biscuits into
smaller pieces to provide more treats for
fewer calories.

Will Work for Food

Cockers are very food motivated. Ask your
puppy to do something—whatever you are
currently teaching—each time you give
her food. Each treat and each meal can be
earned. Have her *sit*, *down*, or *come* to get
her food. This will give you several very
short training sessions each day at meal
and treat times.

Water

Water is critical to life; a dog can last
longer without food than without water.
Your Cocker must have water multiple
times a day. Again, a snood can keep her
ears from getting wet. The water should
be clean, so change it regularly, and clean
out the water bowl, too.

Lead Training

An early lesson for your Cocker is getting acclimated to a collar and a lead.

Put a collar on your puppy for short periods of time to get her accustomed to it. Buckle or quick-clip styles are good starter collars. Make sure it isn't too tight. If she is annoyed by it, distract her with treats or a toy.

When she is comfortable with the collar, attach a lead. Initially, let her decide where to go. You just hold the lead and follow. When she stops, move so that you are standing next to her on her right side, facing the same direction. When she moves, you walk, too, in the same direction.

At some point, she may notice the lead, and pull to get away from it. Just hold the lead and let her pull and fuss. When she sees that it does no good, she'll stop arguing.

On the other hand, she may pull forward, pulling you along on a walk. That's no fun either. When she pulls, stop the walk and stand still. When there is some slack in the lead, maybe because she looked back to see why you stopped, start walking again. When the lead is taut again, stop again. Start only when the lead is slack. She'll learn that she gets to go when she doesn't pull. "Going on the walk" is the fun part for her, and walking her on a loose lead is more fun for you.

If you are going to show your Cocker, she will need to become accustomed to a show collar. These are usually a slip, choke, or martingale style worn high on the neck. A show collar will fit more snugly than a buckle or similar collar, but not choke her. It will take practice for your puppy to get comfortable with a show collar.

The show lead is shorter, maybe three or four feet long, than the typical six-foot walk lead. The show lead is used to help hold the collar higher up on the Cocker's neck. It will take practice for your puppy to learn to walk and trot next to you on the show lead.

Car Travel

The best way for your Cocker to comfortably ride in a car is in a crate. This way the windows can be opened without risk to her of getting hit by anything if she sticks her head out or of her escaping. If you have an accident, even a little one, the jolt can send a loose puppy flying around the car, hurting her or another person in the vehicle. In a crate, she is safe.

Initially, just put her in the crate in the car without driving anywhere. Let her get comfortable with getting in and out. Help her out, especially when her skeletal structure is developing, so that she doesn't injure herself landing on her front legs when jumping from a high place.

Proceed to short drives. Include treats. Some places, like drive-through banks, may offer biscuits for customer's dogs. If you stop and get ice cream, find a way to give your Cocker a taste.

Going in a car should be fun. It should never be only a trip to the groomer who pulls her hair or the veterinarian who gives her shots.

If you don't want your Cocker on your bed when she is older, don't allow her on the bed when she is a puppy.

Handling

You can improve your groomer's and your vet's opinion of your Cocker Spaniel if you get her accustomed to being handled, examined, and groomed. Too many owners don't do this, so that when others try to work with Cockers, the dogs are uncooperative.

Hopefully your breeder handled the puppies a lot; you will be continuing the process. Make the handling fun and pleasurable for her. Start with very short sessions—a minute or less—and include treats while she is getting accustomed to the process. Slowly progress to longer sessions and eventually give the treats only intermittently.

Give her doggy massage. Use soft pressure only for relaxing. Make small circular motions with your fingertips starting with her nose. Keeping your hands on her, progress with the little circles over her whole body. When she is relaxed and if she likes lying on her back, give her gentle belly rubs. Touch her all over, including her ears, lifting her lips to see her teeth, looking at each paw and each nail.

Include grooming in handling. Again, keep the sessions short. Clean one ear, give her a treat, session over. Clip one nail—or pretend to—give her a treat, session over. Progress to two nails, then three. Eventually, she will see the benefits (treats) to getting groomed. Brush her regularly. Work through any tangles gently to get them out. Cockers with tangled hair that gets pulled at the groomer's are understandably disagreeable when someone tries to work on their coat. It is up to you to make sure that her coat stays in good condition.

Don't have preconceived notions of how a Cocker should behave. Your puppy is an individual. Tailor the training to her.

The Cocker is watching her owner, looking for instruction.

You are a team. If you are having training problems, the problem may be at your end of the leash.

Learning doesn't progress evenly. There will be breakthroughs, plateaus, and roadblocks. This is normal. If something isn't working, and you've given it enough time, try a new approach.

Attention

Your Cocker is a busy puppy, with many things to learn and investigate; much can distract her. And like any youngster, she has a short attention span. For the rest of your training to be effective, you need to teach her *attention*. She is paying attention when she is looking at you.

To teach this, put some very tasty treats in each of your closed hands. Kneel or sit on the floor in front of your Cocker so she can easily look at your face. Let your puppy sniff your closed hands so she

knows you have goodies. Hold your hands about two feet apart and a bit higher than your puppy's head. She will try to get the treats from your hands, but don't give her any. Keep her interested, teasing her by letting her sniff the hand-held treats.

She will eventually, accidentally, make eye contact with you. When she looks in

> **COCKER CLUE**
> **Multitasking**
> *You'll be teaching your Cocker many things in the same time period, although you may focus on only one during any single training session. You won't completely finish one lesson before starting another. As a youngster, your puppy may learn attention, sit, what agility equipment looks like, and what birds smell like, all in the same week. She has an amazing capacity to learn, and the more she learns, the more she can learn.*

your eyes for even a second, say "Good girl!" and give her a treat. Each time she makes eye contact, give her a treat and praise her. Alternate treat hands so she doesn't anticipate the hand providing the goody.

Soon she will catch on to the game and stare at you to get the treat. Start attaching a word to the behavior, such as "Watch Me" or "Ready." This is the command you will give her when you want her to pay attention, because you will be giving another command. There is no point in asking her to do something if you don't have her attention.

When you say "Watch Me!," say the command only once, not repeatedly. If her attention starts to stray, entice it back with sounds (like a click or smooching), movement of your hands, a sniff of the treat in your hand. Keep your face happy, with squinty eyes with lots of wrinkles and a smiling mouth. Reinforce with treats.

Initially, release her quickly. Pause, then say "Watch Me!" again. Then, "Good girl!," release, and treat. Stand up straight, don't bend over when releasing. Give the treat after the release so that they don't see the treat as the release, and also because they will then focus on the treat, not on you.

Gradually increase the time you keep her attention on you. The goal is to have her look to you for direction.

Release

It is useful to have a word that releases your dog from the current command. This lets her know that she can move or do something else. It is usually a release from a *stay* command. Many trainers use the word "Okay," meaning the dog can get up from the *down* or *sit* position.

Leave It

Leave it is another useful command. It means, don't touch the item, probably on the floor, that the puppy wants. It might be a bit of food, a toy, or an electric cord.

Patience and Self-Control

Your puppy can learn all sorts of useful commands—*sit*, *down*, and more—as well as activities such as obedience and agility. But part of maturity is learning patience and self-control.

Don't give a demanding dog what it is demanding. Your Cocker is not the one who decides when to play with you and when to insist upon attention. If you want to accommodate her request for a game or petting, ask her to do something first, such as *sit* or whatever she has been learning. Her reward for performing is the game or cuddling.

If your puppy has a tantrum, wait it out. Don't give in and reward bad behavior. Wait until she stops protesting, then reward her with a treat or praise. If she protests gentle grooming, tell her "No!" When she is calm and well behaved, praise and offer a goody. Keep calm and quiet yourself; don't add to your dog's arousal, making it worse.

Teach *sit–stay* as a method to help your puppy learn self-control and patience.

5 Concepts for Training Your Cocker Spaniel

There have been many different techniques, methods, and philosophies for training dogs over the years. Before further discussing teaching specific behaviors, let's review the current concepts and principles that should underlie all training methods to make them more effective. How well your dog learns depends on many things: your relationship with each other, how completely and accurately you observe and understand your Cocker, and how effective your communication is, including your attitudes, timing, and physical behaviors.

Cocker Temperament

Dogs have many characteristics in common simply because they are dogs. They are social creatures with common communication, emotions, and thought processes. Selection and breeding have produced dog breeds that are strong in certain physical, behavioral, and temperament characteristics. Herding dogs work livestock. Hounds hunt fur-bearing animals. And sporting breeds locate game birds for the hunter and retrieve the downed birds.

The Cocker Spaniel is the smallest sporting breed and has many characteristics common to dogs in general and to sporting dogs in particular, as well as traits that define spaniels and the Cocker Spaniel. Consider the typical Cocker temperament when training your dog. A well-bred Cocker is a merry, happy spaniel with a strong attachment to people. He is a high-energy dog, suitable for endurance in the field, whether he actually goes hunting or not. He has a great capacity to learn. In fact, the more you teach your Cocker, the greater his ability to learn even more. Cockers tend to have a softer temperament, so harsh or rough training methods don't work with them.

Cockers are social dogs and have a strong need to be with their family. They can be very sensitive to sounds and movements; rough handling isn't effective with Cockers. They can be excitable, especially when they don't get enough exercise. While bred to work fairly close to the hunter, some may still run off if something attracts their interest.

Poorly-bred Cockers can be shy or sub-missive, sharp, aggressive, protective of their food or toys, and may have problems with submissive urination. Some of these will affect your training methods. Aggression and guarding are also problems that training can mitigate or manage.

Besides characteristics of dogs and of the breed, your Cocker will also have his own individual temperament. Some are bright and learn quickly, while others are stubborn. The bright ones will learn easily; don't bore them with endless repetition. With a stubborn puppy, you as trainer need to be more stubborn than the dog, and patient, but persistent.

Some Cockers are extroverts; others are introverts. Socializing is easier with extroverts. Introverts need more time to feel comfortable around new people, places, and other dogs. Some dogs don't like to be hugged by strangers, and that is okay.

Just as you have your unique personality, so does your puppy, which should be enjoyed, respected, and loved.

Many dogs in the same family look very much alike but have different personalities, just like members of your family.

How Cockers Learn

Dogs are simple. Like us, they do what feels good and avoid what feels bad. As youngsters, when everything is new, they experiment with many behaviors. Some behaviors are inherently fun, like running, chewing, and digging, and will be continued whether you encourage them or not. Other activities, many we don't even notice, are tried and abandoned as unrewarding or unpleasant.

Your challenge and opportunity are to make the behaviors you want him to do feel good. Further, you can make the activities you don't want your Cocker to pursue either unavailable or unpleasant. You need to be in control.

Your Cocker's temperament will affect the methods that work best with him. The confident, happy dog is the most receptive to training. The puppy has a shorter attention span than an experienced dog accustomed to learning. The easily distracted dog needs help to focus. The soft, sensitive dog needs gentle handling. Some dogs are more stubborn, which will require more patience and persistence on your part. Understand your dog, and modify your methods where necessary to fit his individual personality.

COCKER CLUE

Your Cocker's stage of life can affect what and how he learns, and should be considered as you train. Note that some of the stages overlap.

- *Neonatal—0 to 13 days. The ability to experience mild physical stress enables puppies to learn and handle stress better.*
- *Transition—13 to 21 days. As eyes and ears open, puppies can learn about different stimuli that they can feel, see, taste, and smell.*
- *Awareness—21 to 23 days. Rapid sensory development makes this an ideal stage to introduce new surfaces and new sounds.*
- *Canine socialization—21 to 49 days. Puppies learn how to be a dog and be part of a pack. Add a variety of household noises.*
- *Human socialization—7 to 12 weeks. Puppies are introduced to a wide variety of experiences, including simple training. Socialization to a wide variety of people and places and other friendly animals can have a significant impact.*
- *Fear period—8 to 10 weeks. Traumatic experiences can have a lasting effect.*

Ensure that the puppy's experiences are positive.

- *Flight instinct period—4 to 8 months. Puppies will test some limits, including not responding when called. Keep the leash on.*
- *Second fear period—6 to 14 months. Adolescence brings some fear of new situations. Ignore your dog's concerns and let him figure out that he need not be afraid. He may again test the boundaries. Reinforce the limits and rules.*
- *Young adulthood—18 to 24 months. Some dogs become more aggressive during this time and more protective. He may test whether he can take over as leader. Remind him of your status with leader behavior.*
- *Adulthood—2 to 3 years to approximately 10 years. Analogous to 20 to 30 human years in age.*
- *Senior citizen—ten plus years. Old dogs can learn new tricks. But consider their lower energy level and some physical limitations, including less acute hearing and sight, arthritis, and other aches and pains.*

Communication

You have choices on how you communicate with your Cocker Spaniel; some ways are much more productive than others. The most effective methods, which also can produce the most successful training results, mirror those used by dogs with each other.

Your dog is already watching you, trying to figure out "meanings" to what you do. Have you noticed that when he hears you get the dog biscuit box from the cupboard that he runs to you to get a cookie? When you put on your walking shoes, does he dance around anticipating a walk? Your Cocker has "learned" that certain cues from you indicate certain results. It is up to you to use cues deliberately to elicit the behaviors you want.

Tone of Voice

Tone of voice is very meaningful to your Cocker Spaniel, like the sounds dogs make to speak to each other. It is much more important than what you are saying. You can recite the alphabet, but the dog will hear significantly different messages depending on how you say it. A happy, excited, high-pitched tone relays joy, playfulness, and approval. Conversely, a gruff, mean, low-pitched voice conveys disapproval, threat, and correction. Women with higher pitched voices can consciously lower their voices when correcting their dogs, while men, with deeper voices, should pitch their tones higher to encourage and praise so the dog won't misunderstand the message.

If your Cocker is overly excitable, don't let your voice add to the excitement. Keep your tone friendly and calm, not high-pitched and fast. A puppy that is too revved up can't focus. If your Cocker is submissive or shy, temper your correction voice so that you don't add to his apprehension.

Commands are given in a firm tone of voice. You aren't asking your Cocker to do something; you are telling him. While your tone is firm, it doesn't need to be loud. Your dog has sensitive hearing; you don't need to shout at him to be understood.

Words

During training, you will attach words to certain behaviors that your Cocker will learn. Stick to one- or two-syllable words, rather than phrases or sentences. *Down* is better than *lie down*. Be consistent and use the same command every time to ask for the behavior you want. The whole family must use the same verbal commands, also. Say, *"Come!"* when you want your dog to come to you, rather than *"Come!"* sometimes, *"Here!"* at others, or *"Come here puppy."*

Hand Signals

Hand signals can reinforce words as you are training. This is equivalent to giving two commands at once. Subsequently,

Before you can effectively communicate with your Cocker, he must be looking at you and paying attention.

you should be able to use either voice commands or hand signals. When first using hand signals, make them broad and definite so that your Cocker can see unequivocally what the movement is. Be consistent with your hand signals, as you are with words, for your puppy can get confused if you don't give the same hand signal every time you want a given behavior.

Your Cocker is especially alert to movement and therefore can be very receptive to hand signals. Depending on the activities you train him for, hand signals may be easier to see or faster to deliver.

> **COCKER CLUE**
> *The leader owns the space; the follower gets out of the path of the leader. Use your body to block your dog when he is moving in a direction you don't want him to. Nudge him, gently, out of the way with your body by walking into him so he has to move. Don't step on him. This isn't a correction. It is a way to move your dog in a way that reinforces your leader position.*

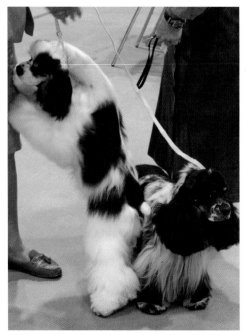

Your Cocker will take cues from your attitude and mood. Whether you are self-assured and happy or nervous and anxious, it will go right down the lead to your dog.

Body Language

Dogs communicate with each other using body language. People do too. You can send meaning to your dog with your body. Dogs can detect even slight differences, so be aware of the messages you send.

Your "message" includes your face and expression. Smile and look happy when training and praising your dog. Wrinkle your face with smiles to indicate your approval. Dogs notice even an eighth of an inch (or less) change in your smile, eyes, or brows; they can see those slight differences in other dogs' faces, too. Scowl when correcting your dog to reinforce your tone of voice. People and dogs recognize the meaning of a grimace. Exaggerate your frown to show your displeasure.

Leader Posture

You are your Cocker's leader so stand like one. When you are training, stand and walk tall and proudly, shoulders back, self-assured. Your dog will look to you. If he is confident of your leadership, he is more likely to follow and respond. On the other hand, if you stand and walk with poor posture, meekly and lacking confidence, your puppy will not consider you a suitable leader, and may even promote himself to leader of your pack.

A person's tall, erect posture indicates leadership and power to a dog. If your puppy is unsure of your friendly overtures, you can crouch down, which makes you smaller and less threatening. Conversely, dominant dogs come down over the top of lower-ranked dogs. You might intend your leaning over your Cocker to hug him as a friendly, loving gesture. But a dog may interpret it as assertive or aggressive.

Touch

Dog-to-dog touch can be friendly or threatening. Usually, dog-to-human touch is an attempt to get closer or to get attention. Pay attention and see what he wants.

Much human-to-dog touch is positive. Most dogs enjoy stroking and gentle scratching. Patting the top of the head isn't as appealing to your dog, however. Look at his expression and see if he is enjoying your attention. If your intention is friendly, make sure your overtures are welcomed and pleasurable for your Cocker.

On the other hand, if your intent is correction, don't strike or hit your dog. Hitting is ineffective, and you are teaching your dog by example to be aggressive.

If you need to correct a dog, to make a stronger impression, do so as a mother dog would correct her puppies. One technique that can be used if the puppy is mouthing someone inappropriately is to grasp his muzzle and say "No!" When taking his

muzzle in your hand, come up from underneath his head to avoid his becoming hand shy. Hold the muzzle on your palm with your thumb and fingers wrapped around the top of his muzzle.

Another correction can be used if you find the puppy doing something inherently dangerous, like chewing an electric cord, and you need to make a strong impression. You can hold your puppy by the scruff of the neck and give him a little shake, just enough to startle him and show him electric cords are no fun at all. This sterner correction is for potentially dangerous situations. If you just want the puppy not to touch something, like the newspaper or your shoes, you can use the *leave it* command.

Rewarding Your Cocker

Encourage your Cocker to learn by rewarding him when he does something right. You can offer words of praise and a scratch behind the ear.

Would you work for just words of appreciation and a pat on the back? No sirree! You want a paycheck! Your dog wants more reward, too, and will work much harder to get it. A reward for your Cocker is a treat, something he really loves. This treat can both be used to guide your puppy into the behavior you want and also to reward him when he does it.

For some undiscriminating dogs, pieces of dog biscuits will do. But for others, you need to raise the stakes (or steaks). Meat is always a favorite, perhaps with a bit of

39

garlic flavor sprinkled on if your dog likes that seasoning. Hard cheese is tasty. Experiment to see what really excites your Cocker.

One way to have a supply of treats available is to keep an eye on your own leftovers. A leftover pork chop, an end piece or two of roast, some bits of steak (not fat or gristle) that you didn't finish can be cut into small pieces, tossed in a plastic sandwich bag, and put in the freezer for future use. These treats provide doggy "paychecks" for future training sessions.

You can use regular meals as reinforcers, too. "Puppy, do you want your dinner?" Before every meal, have him do one or two of the behaviors, such as *sit* or *down*, that you are working on before giving him the food. Wait until he does the command, release your Cocker ("Okay!"), and give him his meal. Your Cocker can illustrate the maxim "Will work for food!"

Shaping Behavior

In addition to being a reward, the treat can be an inducement to do the behavior. You can use the food as a lure to produce the behavior.

To have your dog *sit*, hold the treat an inch above his nose. As he tips his muzzle up, move the treat up a little higher and a little back. As he lifts his head, his rear will lower. Reward the lowering of his rear since it is going in the direction of the *sit*. You are guiding his body motion with the bait. With repeated attempts, reward increasingly lower positions of his bottom until his fanny hits the floor.

When he has learned the command, you can tell him to *sit* before getting the

COCKER CLUE

Ever notice on televised dog shows that the handlers are holding treats that fascinate the dogs, treats that they give their dogs once in awhile? For the most part, that treat is liver, cooked in a manner so that it is easy to handle and can be put in one's pocket without mess. Here is the recipe.

One pound sliced beef liver
Garlic powder
Paper plates (dinner-sized)

- *Rinse the liver under cold water until the water runs clear.*
- *Place the liver pieces in a single layer on a double layer of paper plates.*
- *Sprinkle with garlic powder.*
- *Use another paper plate to cover the liver.*
- *Microwave the liver for 6 minutes on high.*
- *Turn the liver over on the double plate; cover again with the third plate.*
- *Microwave the liver for 2 more minutes on high.*
- *Cool and place in a food storage bag and freeze.*
- *Defrost and use as necessary.*

When giving this treat to your Cocker, only give very tiny pieces, about 1/4 inch on a side. Feeding too much liver as treats may upset his tummy, so use only small amounts. Cooked chicken and string cheese are also very appealing treats for training.

COCKER CLUE

Food isn't the only reward that your Cocker enjoys. Play and toys can serve that function too. At the end of a training session, reward him with his favorite toy, a game of tug of war, his Frisbee, or a ball to fetch.

Try different treats to see what your Cocker likes best. Use that treat to motivate and reward him for learning.

treat. Later, you can treat only for a greater level of precision, such as a straight sit by coaxing him into the desired position with your hand, body, and lure, giving the goody when he does the behavior you are looking for.

Intermittent Reinforcement

Once your Cocker has learned the behavior you are teaching, you need not reward him every time. Provide the treat every second or third time instead and eventually even less often. This is called "intermittent" reinforcement, and it is very effective in maintaining the behaviors you have taught. Your Cocker is even more eager, for maybe this time he'll get the goody!

Note that intermittent reinforcement is used only after your Cocker knows and performs the command reliably. When he knows the behavior well and also knows that he doesn't get the treat every time, he will still respond when you don't have the treat handy.

Corrections

While rewards are one of the biggest tools in your training arsenal, corrections are an option, too. It produces a negative (from your Cocker's point of view) result when he does an action, hopefully causing him to avoid that action in the future. The best are when the situation provides a "correction," rather than you.

Here are some examples of results you can arrange that will discourage certain behaviors in your puppy.

■ Put a bad tasting product on an item that you don't want your dog to chew. If he chews it, he gets a nasty taste in his mouth. Note that it must be a bad taste from your Cocker's point of view. Some things we think are horrid are appealing to dogs. Some nasty tastes are commercially available for discouraging dogs, often bitter citrus flavors. You can also use hot pepper sauce.

- Your doing an about-turn when walking your dog and he is pulling ahead of you corrects your Cocker. Do the about-turn when he is a full-body length ahead of you, but the lead isn't yet taut. Since he wasn't watching, he gets pulled in the changed direction. You didn't cause his problem. It occurred because he wasn't paying attention when you changed direction. Be careful to adjust how abrupt the direction change is to the age and size of your Cocker. You are startling your dog, not jerking him off his feet.
- He jumps up on you and you grab his paws, and hold them. He's trapped. He'll jump, but not close enough for you to grab his paws.

This is what you want to see when you call your Cocker: an immediate, happy, eager-to-get-to-you response.

Timing

Timing is everything, and it certainly is critical in training your Cocker. You must reward the behavior when, or immediately after, it happens for your puppy to understand what the reward is for. Conversely, the correction must happen when the action is happening, or your dog won't associate it with the problem behavior. If you discover that your puppy has chewed the chair leg, but isn't doing it now, it is totally useless to correct him. Further, you gave him access to the chair leg and weren't supervising, so the fault may be yours.

Use the three-second rule. The reward or correction must happen within three seconds or less to be effective. After that, your puppy may connect the reward or punishment to something else. The puppy must still be involved in or immediately concluding the behavior to be rewarded or corrected. If he has progressed to something else, he won't understand what you want or don't want.

Sometimes, you can see your Cocker considering doing something wrong. He is looking at furniture he's not allowed on and preparing to jump up. He's looking at the cat and preparing to pounce. Say a stern "No!" before he does it—correct the *thought*, which is more effective than correcting the behavior itself.

Timing is also a part of giving commands. Attach the command name to the behavior when the dog is doing the behavior (not after he has done it) so he can make the association of the behavior and the word. Make certain that your dog is paying attention and looking at you

If you have more than one dog, and one isn't interested in his lessons, put him somewhere where he can watch you work with the other dog. He will see that he is missing the fun and attention, and he will be more cooperative when it is his turn again.

before giving a command. If his attention is elsewhere, he won't respond. But the fault is yours, not his; you need his attention first.

After you have attached the word to the behavior and your dog understands, you should give the command once, and not repeat it if your dog has heard. Saying "Sit, sit, sit, sit, sit, sit" multiple times becomes nagging, and your Cocker will tune it out. Say the command once and show him the treat he will get if he does it. He may think for a minute or two or more, but he will figure out what he needs to do to get the goody.

Short Sessions

Quick, short lessons are the most effective for your Cocker. Instead of a daily thirty-minute training session, have ten three-minute sessions or fifteen two-minute lessons. Show him the behavior, get him to do it, give him the treat, a lot of praise and petting, and go on to whatever else you are doing.

This method keeps the sessions fun and avoids making it feel like work for both of you. Longer sessions are tiring, repetitious, and boring for both of you. Keep treats handy so you can sprinkle training throughout the day or evening. Every interaction with your Cocker is a training opportunity, where you can encourage the behavior you like and discourage inappropriate behavior.

Distractions

Your Cocker may perform in your home and yard. But he is not really trained until he will obey commands in different places and with distractions.

Kids and Cockers go together, but it will be hard for your puppy to concentrate on new lessons when children are playing nearby.

Once your dog is reliable in your normal training places, practice with him in other places. Keep him on lead for safety. Practice with other people, children, and dogs around, so that he learns to pay attention only to you. Other people can help provide distractions. When your dog can perform dependably with distractions, then he is truly trained.

When you introduce distractions, start with low-level distractions and progress to mid- and higher-level distractions when possible. The distraction level is modified by distance and movement. Another dog two blocks away is less distracting to your puppy than one two feet away. A child standing still attracts less attention than one running or throwing a ball. You won't

be able to practice in every possible situation, but the more different conditions your dog can practice in, the more reliable he will be with additional new ones.

Clicker Training

A clicker is a small metal toy, sometimes used in games, and sometimes called a cricket because of the clicking sound it makes. Clicker training is used to mark with the "click" sound your Cocker's action that you want to praise and reward. When the dog does what you ask, you click. Then you praise and give the treat. Your dog understands that the click sound means, "This is what you want me to do to get the reward" and "The treat is coming!" The faster the food follows the click, the faster the dog will understand that the click means food.

The click is more effective than your saying a word or making a sound to mark the behavior. The click has a more consistent sound. The click sound doesn't occur accidentally in conversation as other words or sounds you might use.

The first step is to associate the click sound with treats. Prepare a bowl of extra special treats cut into very small pieces— meat or cheese work well. They should be soft and small so the dog can eat them quickly. In a quiet area, so your Cocker can hear the click, click the clicker and give him a treat. Then click it again and give another treat. You aren't training him to do anything at this point. You are just connecting the food with the click.

When you are training, you can use the clicker to mark the exact point where you want to reward the behavior, for instance, the instant his fanny hits the floor for a *sit* command. Your Cocker associates the click with a treat. He knows the treat is coming when he hears the click. You can make the clicker sound more quickly and at a more precise moment than you can get food to his mouth. Your puppy will learn quickly because he will know exactly what he is doing when he gets the click. He will learn that behavior faster to get the click, which in turn means there is a treat for him. Especially at the beginning, give your puppy the treat as soon after the click as possible.

Practice reading your Cocker's body posture and expression. This puppy seems unsure and anxious.

Reading Your Cocker's Behavior

Just as your Cocker reads your body language, your should look for and recognize his. Understanding what he is thinking and feeling lets you adjust your training to suit him.

Look at your dog's posture. If he is standing tall with neck arched, he is confident and unafraid. If he is crouching, even a little, with his head lowered, he is apprehensive or fearful. The neck and head positions are important parts of posture. Weight distribution and leaning also have meaning. A dog leaning forward with more weight on his front legs is confident and may be angry. Turning away and having more weight on the rear legs indicate that the dog is less secure or comfortable.

Dogs' ears can be very expressive, but there are fewer ear movements to see with the long drop-ears of Cocker Spaniels. Still, there are muscles on the head that can, when tensed, create the slightest lift at the base of the ears. This is the equivalent to a breed with erect ears having the ears stand stiffly upright. The dog is alert, focused, and paying attention.

Tails are eloquent indicators of emotion, whether they are docked or not. Natural carriage, up or down, will vary with the breed. Cocker tails are normally carried level with the back or slightly higher. A nervous or fearful dog's tail will be kept down, clamped against its body. When your Cocker is happy, his tail will be wagging gaily.

Hair, too, can show your dog's angry feelings. The hairs stand on end when he perceives a threat that he needs to defend against. It can be seen if the hairs are fairly short on the back, but is less visible with long hair. The hair standing up can make the dog look larger, and therefore more threatening, to an opponent.

Eyes are the windows of your dog's soul. You can see if he feels happy, sad, tired, nervous, and many other emotions. Confident dogs will maintain eye contact as will loving dogs. If your dog feels subordinate to a dominant being, which could be you, another person, or another dog, he will look away.

Muzzle and lips are expressive on a dog just as your lower face and mouth are on you. A happy, comfortable dog may smile. His face is relaxed, his mouth may be open, with the corners of the mouth pulled back. An angry dog may lift his lips and display his teeth in a warning gesture. The upset dog may tense his face, the corners of his

> **COCKER CLUE**
>
> *Notice your Cocker's reactions to your training techniques. Does he respond well to treats? If not, try a more delicious treat. Or make sure he hasn't eaten recently. You may need to reward him with something else, such as a toy or playtime. If he doesn't understand what you are trying to communicate, examine your methods to make sure you are being clear and consistent and "talking" in a language he can understand. He can't read your mind. Look at your dog's responses to see what you are doing, right or wrong.*

mouth are not pulled back, and his lips may purse.

Dogs have gestures that have specific meanings. One of the most common is the play bow. Your dog will put his forelegs flat on the floor with his rump up high in the air. He is inviting you or whoever he is with, including another dog, to come play with him. An exaggerated poke with a front leg is also an invitation to play.

Leader of the Pack

Dogs are pack animals, and it is important that you are and that your dog sees you as the leader of the pack. This doesn't mean that you have to be harsh, demanding, or mean; it doesn't mean that your relationship with your dog is less loving. Training through intimidation doesn't work.

The leader in a dog pack is the one in control, who decides what to do, and who does what first. The leader has special freedom and priority in having desirable resources. Your Cocker will see you as leader if you are in control, if you make the decisions and, when important, you go first. Your dog recognizes leadership behavior. Use your leadership to organize the training so that your dog cannot fail and can only succeed. You control the food and the toys, you can open doors, you are the leader.

One big item you have control of is food. After all, you provide it! Don't serve your dog as though you are a waiter. Make it a big deal. Let him see you prepare it. In the wild, the leader eats first. You might even eat a cracker slowly while you make him wait for his food to emphasize the point. Have him do some behavior that you are working on, such as *sit* or *down*, before he gets the meal. Then, when he has waited and worked for the food, you can give it to him. Put the food on the floor and give him your release command ("*Okay!*") before letting him eat.

You also control the treats. Your puppy shouldn't get a treat when he begs for one; that puts him in control. He should get it when you decide, and he should do something for you, such as *sit* or *down*, to get it. Call him to you several times during the day, and give him a treat when he comes. But when he comes to you and demands a treat, don't give the goody; acquiescing to his demands makes your Cocker the pack leader.

You are also in charge of the toys and games. You should initiate playtime. Keep a special toy away from your puppy until you decide it is time for a game. Get the toy and play with him. Then, before he

Your Cocker will more readily learn from and follow you when he has confidence in your leadership.

gets bored and quits the game, you end the game and put the toy away. You are in charge.

When appropriate, you go first. Go down a hall first; go through a door first.

Remember your posture, too. Stand and act like you are the pack leader.

The leader is also the winner. When you tell your Cocker to do something, you need to be able to make it happen. If you cannot or do not, your puppy wins. If you tell your puppy not to do something, and he does it without repercussion, he wins. Your puppy keeps score. If you have many

more points than he does, then he will recognize that you are, indeed, the leader.

Control your temper. If you are upset for any reason, don't begin a training session. If you get angry, training is over.

Your Cocker will be most happy and comfortable when he has a competent pack leader he can look up to, follow, and have confidence in—you!

What Not to Do

While concentrating on what to do to improve your training success, watch that you don't do things that will impede progress.

The old yank-and-jerk-on-the-collar methods of training have been discredited, so don't use them, and don't work with trainers who train primarily through punishment. Don't use dominance or aggression to teach your Cocker. You won't train your dog by abusing him.

When reinforcing a behavior, make sure the reward is on time and sufficient. Don't correct your puppy at the wrong time, that is, after the behavior has been done. He won't know what he is being punished for. Don't ever, ever call your dog to you to correct him, no matter what he has done. All you will accomplish is teaching him not to come to you.

COCKER CLUE
Cockers are sensitive. They experience emotions. They can feel fear, uncertainty, anxiety, enthusiasm. They can be energetic or tired or have aches and pains. They can have good days and bad ones. Consider how your Cocker is feeling when training. Skip some training sessions if the results are likely to be negative and leave a bad impression. Take advantage of the good days to include more training sessions.

6 *Socialization*

The purpose of socializing your Cocker Spaniel is to have a confident, cosmopolitan dog, comfortable around different people, other dogs, and other animals in a variety of places and situations. It is done by providing her with as many positive experiences as possible with all sorts of people, places, and things.

The most critical period for socialization is between eight and sixteen weeks. During this period, experiences will have the most impact. Something new and pleasant each day, however small, is the goal. But socialization must be done before and after this age as well. The more you invest in this part of your puppy's education, the greater will be your rewards throughout her life.

Each Cocker is born with her own temperament and disposition. You won't turn a reserved Cocker into the life of the party or a high-energy puppy into a lazy slug. But with early and continuous socialization, you can help ensure that your Cocker will be comfortable in a variety of situations, have appropriate social skills with people and animals, and be an amiable companion you can enjoy taking with you.

Consider your Cocker's innate temperament when introducing her to new things. Let her investigate at her own speed. Some dogs will be very curious and will eagerly approach the unfamiliar. Others are more cautious and will hesitate. Watch for signs of anxiety, such as ears laid back, tail tucked, leaning away or on you. Nervous dogs may lick their lips excessively or lick their noses with their tongues. They may look at what they are concerned about, but pull away; they may yawn. Don't push. Be confident yourself; she will look to you as a role model to see how she should react. If she is concerned or afraid, don't pet and coo over her; that will reinforce her anxiety. Ignore it, and let her get over it by seeing and learning that there is nothing to fear.

Make sure all the new experiences are positive ones. It is up to you to prescreen them to make certain she will have a pleasant time. Look at it from your Cocker's point of view. Don't ask her to encounter too many new things at once which could overwhelm her. Make sure that dogs that she meets are friendly and won't or cannot jump on her. If one does, even with playful good intentions, she can be traumatized and react aggressively to similar dogs in the future.

Initial Socialization

Ideally, your breeder began the socialization process when the puppies were born. Even before the puppies' eyes were open,

the breeder handled them often. Small stresses encountered at a very young age can produce puppies that can better handle stress when they are older. Puppies can be held vertically, tilted with their heads down, positioned belly up. They can have their feet tickled and be placed for a few seconds on different surfaces.

As they grow with their mother and littermates, puppies learn how to be dogs. Their mother may teach them that she eats first, and not to stick their noses in her food. She'll show them where to potty. Just as with humans, some moms are more lenient while others are more strict. Puppies will learn to play with their brothers and sisters. And when they bite too hard, even in play, their littermates will protest loudly.

The breeder also introduced different noises, which you should continue. Music, vacuum cleaners, television, banging and clanging of pots, toys, and other household objects should all be familiar to your puppy. Breeders let people visit the puppies, including children, senior citizens, whomever can be recruited to play with the litter. Different surfaces, such as wood, concrete, carpet, tile, grass are also introduced. All these add to the puppies' store of experiences.

People to Meet

You can continue the socialization process. Begin by introducing your Cocker to your family, neighbors, and friendly neighborhood pets. Consider the relative size of the other pets. Don't let your puppy bully a small animal, nor be frightened by a large one.

Carry tiny treats with you and encourage new people whom your puppy meets to offer them to her. She'll conclude that strangers are a source of wonderful goodies. Include the mailman, meter reader, and tradespeople, as well as visitors to your house to her widening circle of friends. When she is brave and plays with new or recently met children or dogs, give her a treat. When she exhibits friendly, appropriately social behavior, give her a treat. You are rewarding attitude and behavior just as if you were training *sit* or *down*.

As she meets new folks, have them touch, pet, and examine her. Your Cocker needs to be comfortable being handled by you and by others. Touch her ears, her tail, her feet. Stroke her body. Make is pleasurable. It will help her become more at ease with grooming and visits to the veterinarian. If she will be in dog shows, have people look at her teeth as judges will do in the show rings.

Have her meet different people, including smaller children and very large or tall

Introduce your Cocker to as many different children as you can find, from very young to teenagers, especially if you don't have children in your household.

adults. Include folks of different races and nationalities. Have some wear hats, big coats, or sunglasses. Recruit men with beards and mustaches. Have others carry umbrellas, shopping parcels, or other pets. Meeting people on crutches, in wheelchairs, and with walkers will acclimate her to different experiences. Children on bikes, roller skates, or skateboards can offer treats, too.

Listen Up!

Add to the sounds your Cocker encounters. Doorbells and ringing phones, lawn mowers, power tools, and traffic sounds can be

Make sure the beach allows dogs before bringing your Cocker.

Places to Go

Take your Cocker with you to the many places that allow dogs. Make it fun, but never for so much or so long that she becomes tired or stressed. The neighborhood and nearby parks are good places to start. Include short car trips.

Training classes are excellent places to meet new people and dogs. Your Cocker can participate in puppy kindergarten classes and dog show handling classes. She can sit on the sidelines and watch other classes. Dogs learn by watching other dogs, and she will likely become eager to join in the activity.

Many pet superstores welcome pets on lead. Some beaches allow dogs. Visit a grooming salon—even if you plan to do your own grooming. Include wide-open spaces and crowded ones. Have her learn how to navigate stairs and ride in an elevator. Visit a nice kennel, and progress to her staying a few hours and even overnight without you. You may need to board her one day. If she enjoys it as a youngster, she will be less stressed than she would be if her first visit occurs when she is older.

Different places will have different smells, something very important to a dog. They will also have different surfaces for your puppy to experience. Make certain that all the experiences your Cocker has are pleasant. Unpleasant and traumatic experiences that a puppy has can have long-lasting negative affects. Make new adventures a game; bring toys as well as treats. Each dog is different. Watch your puppy and see what works for her.

introduced until she ignores them. Give her treats when the sounds happen, so they are associated with something pleasant. Give treats during thunderstorms, but make sure that you don't treat, reward, or reinforce nervous reactions to sounds. Pet and treat when she is ignoring or distracted from the noise.

If you plan to show your Cocker, let her hear clapping and cheering. A future hunting dog should be accustomed to gunfire. See Chaper 14, "Hunt and Field," for more information on this.

Home Schooling

Therapy Dogs

Cocker Spaniels are very social dogs and love people; they also love the attention they get in return. If your Cocker has this typical temperament and you are willing, share her with others who love dogs, but cannot have one by making her a therapy dog.

What Is a Therapy Dog?

"Animal assisted therapy" or "visiting dog" are two of the other terms used for this service. Therapy dogs go with their owners to hospitals, nursing homes, schools, or any facility where people who cannot keep animals enjoy having visits from dogs. Studies have shown that petting a dog reduces stress, lowers blood pressure, and brings smiles to faces of people who might not have many reasons to do so. The visiting dogs often bring back memories of animals they once owned and loved.

Therapy dogs can also visit children. They may attend schools to help teach responsible dog ownership. Some are used as "reading" dogs; children read to the dogs to help build confidence. Dogs are almost always interested in a good story.

Who Can Be a Therapy Dog?

There are many therapy dog organizations. Each certifies and registers dogs meeting certain qualifications. The dogs must be current on their vaccinations and be certified healthy by a veterinarian. They are evaluated to verify that they pass the Canine

Good Citizen program (see Chapter 11) or similar tests. The dogs must be well socialized and well-behaved with people and other dogs. The dogs must balance calmness and friendliness. They cannot be disturbed around walkers, wheelchairs, or other equipment that patients may use. The therapy organizations usually provide identification for certified dogs, such as identification cards and tags for collars.

Therapy groups typically welcome all types of dogs, both purebred and mixed breeds. Some may be from rescue. Some groups are open to other animals as well, including cats and even miniature horses.

Rules for Being a Therapy Dog

Most organizations provide rules for the owner and dog teams to conform to on their visits. These usually require that a certain number of visits be completed to maintain certification with the group. Each dog must be accompanied by a responsible adult. Dogs and owners must be clean and well groomed for each visit and the dogs must be on lead and under control at all times. Some of the groups provide limited insurance for the therapy dog activities.

How Can My Cocker Spaniel Become a Therapy Dog?

To get started, socialize your Cocker thoroughly as described in Chapter 6. Make sure she is comfortable around people and other dogs. Teach her basic obedience, including *sit*, *down*, and *stay*. She will need to come when called.

When you are confident of her temperament and behavior, you can contact a ther-

If your Cocker enjoys meeting new people, being loved and petted, and can be calm in new situations, she has a suitable temperament to become a therapy dog.

apy dog organization and inquire about their rules and procedures and how to become certified. Check several as there may be a group already operating in your area. Established groups will already have places they visit regularly. Often, multiple handlers and their dogs visit together.

If you can't find a functioning group in your area, don't let that stop you. Many nursing homes, children's homes, and assisted living facilities welcome therapy dog visits. After your Cocker is certified, call the activity director of a local facility and ask to visit with your Cocker. They will likely be quite pleased with your offer, meet with you, and schedule regular visits.

What Does a Therapy Dog Do?

On your first few visits, a staff member will take you around to visit the residents or clients. After several visits, you may be invited to visit the residents unaccompanied.

If you are visiting children, your Cocker is just the right size for them to reach and pet. Supervise the interaction, since they may not be familiar with how to properly pet and treat a dog. No ear pulling and no hair pulling, please.

Those in wheelchairs may be able to reach down to pet her. Alternatively, your Cocker may stand on her hind legs and rest her front legs on the side of the chair to be stroked and talked to. Some patients are confined to bed. If they invite you to do so, you may put the Cocker on their bed for the visit.

Therapy Dog Organizations

There are local, regional, and national therapy dog groups. Some have similar names, so don't confuse them. Most have their own Web sites, which describe the group, discuss how to become a member, and provide contact information. Some established national therapy groups are

- Therapy Dog Inc.
  www.therapydogs.com
- Therapy Dogs International, Inc.
  www.tdi-dog.org
- Delta Society
  www.deltasociety.org
- Love on a Leash
  www.therapydogs.net
- Paws for Friendship, Inc.
  www.pawsforfriendshipinc.org

If your Cocker is as wonderful as you believe, donate some of your time and share her with others—there will be rewards for both of you.

7 *Sound Body and Mind*

To be all that he can be, your Cocker Spaniel must be in good health. Like temperament, this is influenced by both the genes he inherited from his parents and the care he receives from you and your family. Some conditions are general and apply to all dogs, while other issues are somewhat more common with Cockers and some other breeds. You can improve your chances of avoiding inherited problems by getting a puppy from a breeder who tests for known Cocker problems. The American Spaniel Club recommends testing hips and eyes at a minimum before breeding.

Ears

Cocker Spaniels, with their long glamorous ears, are more prone to ear infections than are dogs with erect or prick ears because air and light cannot easily get to the inside of the ear. Check your Cocker's ears several times a week and clean them weekly and after bathing with an ear-cleaning solution. Make sure the ears are dry; damp ears can more easily become infected. If you like, fasten them up and out of the way until you are certain they are dry, especially after a bath.

If your Cocker shakes his head, scratches or rubs his ears, check the ear flaps, especially the edges, for oily or greasy or crusty spots, a condition known as seborrhea. You can clean these off with a dandruff or veterinarian-recommended medicated shampoo two or three times weekly until clear.

If you cannot resolve the problem, have your Cocker checked by your veterinarian. Medication may be prescribed if there is an infection or inflammation. Ear mites are another cause for scratching (this is more common in puppies than in adults); your veterinarian can provide medication to treat this.

Veterinarian checking a Cocker Spaniel's ear.

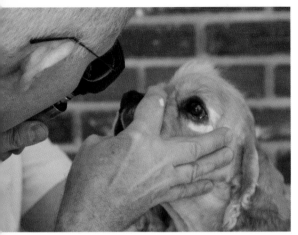

While your veterinarian will examine your Cocker's eyes during his annual checkup, you may also want them examined by a veterinary ophthalmologist.

The medication or ear-flush may be administered at home and will soften any embedded wax too deep for you to remove with normal cleaning. Do this outside, if possible, for your Cocker will shake his head, causing liquid and any debris to go flying. Squirt the prescribed amount of liquid into the ear and massage the base of the ear. When you stop, stand back and allow for your dog to shake. Clean any residual liquid and debris off of the external ear.

Eyes

Keep your Cocker's eyes clean with warm water and ophthalmic solutions or rinses. Don't let shampoo get in his eyes during baths. Check them regularly for any problems.

Ectropion is a common Cocker condition in which the eyelids turn out, often with a drooping lower lid. Dirt, seeds, or other particles can enter this area and inflame or scratch the membranes or other parts of the eye. Ectropion is usually inherited.

Entropion describes lids that turn in towards the eye. The inverted lid or eyelashes rub on the surface of the eye irritating and potentially damaging it. Your veterinarian can determine if these conditions exist and if they are serious enough to warrant action. Entropion may be hereditary or may be the result of inflammation to the conjunctiva, causing swelling and rolling in of the eyelids. Inflammation is easily treated. Your veterinarian may recommend surgery for hereditary entropion.

Cockers may have **distichia** or extra hairs on the edges of the eyelids. They may cause irritation to the eye. Lashes or hairs may be removed, although when the new hairs grow in they may irritate the eyes even more.

Cherry eye describes the enlargement of the tear gland in the corner of the eye, which causes it to break its attachment and flip out of the eye at the base of the third eyelid, which is normally barely visible. It isn't painful, but is unsightful and may be uncomfortable. It can be surgically repaired; consult with your veterinarian.

Dry eye is the result of reduced or absent tear production. It may be caused by cherry eye removal. The eye may redden or have a thick mucous discharge. Have your veterinarian examine and prescribe medication and treatment. Left untreated, the eye can become infected and/or damaged and possibly lead to blindness.

The left eye is normal; the right eye has a cataract.

On the other hand, your Cocker may tear excessively from the corners of his eyes. This may be caused by the tear ducts not opening properly, so that instead of lubricating the eyes' surface, tears drain out of the ducts and out onto the face. Your veterinarian can surgically open the ducts.

Cataracts occur when the lens of the eye becomes so cloudy as to be opaque. It can be surgically removed and an artificial lens inserted. Cataracts are not unusual in very old dogs, but if they occur in young dogs or adults in their prime, there is probably a hereditary component. Cataracts are often categorized by their age of onset, such as juvenile or adult.

Progressive retinal atrophy (PRA) is a set of retinal disorders that can lead to blindness. It may show up as early as four to six months or as late as six to seven years.

It is progressive and affects both eyes. The condition may begin as night or low-light blindness and continue until day blindness sets in. It is inherited and recessive.

Glaucoma is caused by too much fluid in the eye resulting in excess pressure. If not relieved, it can cause permanent damage, leading to blindness. It can occur suddenly and be quite painful. Go to the veterinarian immediately if one or both eyes are red and irritated, and the dog is squinting, or pawing at them. Don't wait for office hours if immediate attention is required to avoid permanent damage to the eye.

Skin Problems

Skin problems can result in tangles and mats in your Cocker's coat formed when your puppy chews and scratches at the irritation. Some bloodlines encounter more skin problems than others, so check with your breeder for information and recommendations. If your Cocker is scratching, chewing, licking, or rubbing, he has a problem that needs your attention.

Seborrhea

Seborrhea is a disorder of the outer layer of the skin, sebaceous glands, and hair follicles in which an excess of cells are created. The result is dry flakes of skin or greasy skin and an odor. Affected dogs may also have chronic waxy ear infections. The condition may be compounded with other bacterial skin infections.

Your veterinarian may recommend using an antiseborrheic shampoo to bathe your Cocker several times a week. The medicated shampoo will have to stay on the skin for 10 to 15 minutes to be effective. This is a long-term solution, for seborrhea can only be managed, not cured. If there is an additional skin infection, other antibiotics may be used to treat it.

Allergies

Dogs can be allergic to many things in their environment. Some allergens may be inhaled; others may be touched or eaten, in the case of food allergies. Allergy symptoms often appear on the skin (reddening and itching) and the dog's scratching and rubbing may result in hair loss. Symptoms are also commonly seen on the ears.

Your Cocker may be allergic to plant materials and grasses, including pollen. Inhaled allergens such as dust, mold, and dander are also common. Food allergies, especially to a particular protein, can cause reactions. Fleas can cause an extreme reaction in a dog allergic to the flea saliva.

Avoidance is often the solution. Prevent fleas and/or switch to a dog food with a different protein source. The most common food allergies are to beef, wheat, and milk products. A fish-based food is a good choice for dogs who develop a reaction to the more common chicken protein in dog foods.

It is harder to avoid all plants and grasses, but reactions to these are usually seasonal. Your veterinarian may recommend an antihistamine. In severe cases, a veterinary dermatologist can do skin allergy tests and recommend allergy injections to desensitize the dog.

Skeletal Problems

Cocker Spaniels are not plagued with the bone and joint problems of some breeds, but you should be aware of a few just to understand what to look for in your own dogs.

Hip Dysplasia is a condition of malformation of the hip joint, where the head of the thigh bone (femur) doesn't fit correctly into the hip socket. The fault can be with the shape of the femoral head, with the shape of the socket, or with their not fitting each other. At the least, the dog will have modeling and eventual arthritis in old age. At worst, it can be crippling and painful, and may be relieved with surgery. This is a condition parents can be tested for, which should reduce the incidence of the condition in their offspring.

Patellar Luxation is a condition where the patella or kneecap luxates, or pops out of place. One or both knees may be affected. The groove in which the kneecap rides may be too shallow, or the muscles and ligaments may not effectively be keeping the patella in place. Toy and smaller

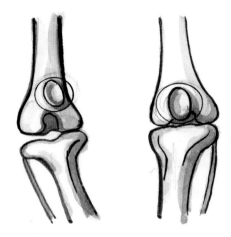

The right patella or kneecap is normal; the left is luxated or out of place.

breeds, including Cockers, may be affected. It can cause pain, cartilage damage, and arthritis. The more severe cases can be corrected with surgery.

If your Cocker has any joint or bone problems, keep his weight down to reduce the stress on the skeleton.

The Orthopedic Foundation for Animals (OFA) maintains a registry of dogs that have been tested for orthopedic diseases and conditions. Their Web site is *www.offa.org*. With a dog's name or AKC number, one can search the OFA database to determine which health screenings a dog has had.

Autoimmune Disorders

Autoimmune disorders are situations in which the body's immune system attacks some part of itself. Cocker Spaniels may have immune mediated hemolytic anemia (IMHA) where the immune system attacks its red blood cells. The cause isn't known, but the disease occurs more in Cockers than other breeds. Symptoms include pale gums, fatigue, and possible jaundice. There is no cure; treatment may include steroids to reduce the immune response.

Cocker Spaniels also have a predisposition for autoimmune thyroiditis. In this disease, the immune system attacks the cells of the thyroid gland. The result is hypothyroidism where the body fails to produce adequate amounts of thyroid hormones. Symptoms include lethargy, weight gain, dry skin, and excessive shedding or hair loss. Treatment includes replacing the thyroid hormone.

Phosphofructokinase Deficiency (PFK)

Phosphofructokinase deficiency is a recessive genetic disease that prevents the

Your veterinarian can check for the stability of the patella (kneecap) and other joints.

metabolism of glucose into energy. The result is that the Cocker has no tolerance for exercise and is likely to be anemic. There is now a DNA test to identify dogs that carry this gene so that they are not bred and thereby will not pass the problem to future generations.

Epilepsy

Epilepsy is a neurological disease. Idiopathic epilepsy is one without a known cause. It seems to have a hereditary component, with multiple genes responsible. Trauma, tumors, nervous system disorders, and hormone problems may also cause seizures.

Seizures may or may not exhibit convulsions, also called grand mal seizures. If you see a dog seizing, keep him away from dangers, including stairs where he might fall and other dogs that might attack. If the seizure lasts more than a few minutes, get the dog to a veterinarian immediately. Even if it is over quickly, get him to the veterinarian as soon as you can. Dogs with a pattern of seizures can be treated with anti-convulsant drugs.

Vaccines and Prevention

Your Cocker Spaniel should have gotten his initial vaccinations from his breeder, and your veterinarian will continue with the protocol. Puppies need regular vaccinations every three weeks, with the last ones of the puppy series given at about four months. After the puppy shots and a

booster a year later, there are one-year and three-year vaccines available to protect against many of the communicable diseases. Your veterinarian will advise you as to which are available and recommended in your area.

Vaccines are categorized today as core and non-core. The core vaccines offer protection against very serious and possibly life-threatening diseases. These include canine parvovirus (CPV), canine distemper virus (CDV), canine adenovirus 2—also referred to as hepatitis—and rabies. Non-core vaccines aren't recommended for all dogs, for the diseases they target are less serious, easily treated, self-limiting, or not as widespread. Included are canine parainfluenza virus (CPiV), bordatella, leptospirosis, giardia, corona, and lyme disease. Many kennels require the bordatella vaccine for kennel cough, as it is very contagious.

Heartworm

If your Cocker has any exposure to mosquitoes, he must be on a heartworm preventive. If a mosquito carrying heartworm bites your dog, the heartworm larvae enter your dog's bloodstream. The larvae develop in the body for several months, ending up as adult heartworms in the dog's heart and lungs. Without treatment, heartworms will kill the dog.

Heartworm treatment is expensive and hard on a dog. It is much better to give your Cocker regular heartworm prevention medication. There are a variety of options available, usually given monthly. They are very effective when given regularly. A dog

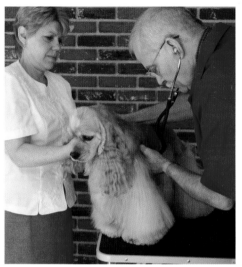

Even if your Cocker gets vaccinations that last for three years, he should get an annual examination that includes the veterinarian listening to his heart and lungs.

that has not been on regular heartworm preventive must be tested for heartworms before starting the preventive.

Parasites—Internal and External

Fleas and ticks are annoying at any time and can also carry disease. For coated dogs, like your Cocker, they can also cause tangles, mats, and hair loss. To get rid of fleas, you must simultaneously treat your dog, your home, and your yard.

Newer products available from your veterinarian are safer than the old poisons once used. Several of these are topical. Imidacloprid is placed on your dog's skin,

spreads over the dog's body, and kills fleas for about a month. Fipronil is applied the same way and will kill fleas and ticks for about a month. Selamectin, also applied in the same manner, kills fleas for a month; it also kills ear mites, some internal parasites, and can be a heartworm preventive.

When treating your home and yard, make certain that the product used not only kills adult fleas, but also kills flea eggs, or prevents them from hatching. If not, two weeks after you treat, you will have a new infestation.

Rubbing alcohol is toxic to both ticks and fleas. If you find a flea on your dog, you can kill it by spraying it with alcohol. If you find a tick on your Cocker, spray it with alcohol first. Then grab it next to the dog's skin with tweezers, or with your hand protected with a tissue. Pull it off slowly so that the head does not detach, and drop into alcohol.

Mites

Mites can also cause problems. Sarcoptic mites can produce sarcoptic mange, an itchy skin disorder. It is contagious and can cause red, itchy spots on people as well. Demodex mites cause demodectic mange. Susceptibility to this condition is inherited.

> **COCKER CLUE**
> **Flea Collar**
> *A flea collar can do double duty in your vacuum cleaner. Cut the collar into short pieces, and put one in the bag. Replace it once a month to kill fleas that get sucked into your vacuum.*

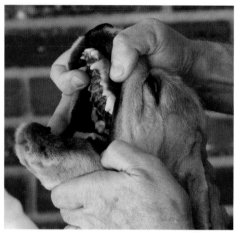

The annual exam will include a veterinary inspection of the mouth, gums, and teeth.

These mites are not contagious to other dogs or people. Both exposures result in hair loss. A skin scraping is needed to diagnose mange. Treatments are available from your veterinarian, usually involving dips, and, possibly, medication.

Intestinal Worms and Infections

Your Cocker puppy will likely have been wormed once or twice before he arrives at your home. He may not need to be wormed again, although his stool should be examined when you visit the veterinarian for his initial checkup and then once a year at his annual exam. The more common worms, hookworms, roundworms, and whipworms, can usually be identified by this test. If you notice segments of tapeworm, which are white and about a quarter or a half inch in length, let your

veterinarian know. Intestinal worms are relatively easy to treat, especially if you do not let your dog get seriously infested. Pick up your dog's stool and dispose of it to help avoid spreading worms.

When your Cocker has diarrhea that continues, have your veterinarian examine a stool sample. It may be one of the worms described above. It may also be coccidia or giardia, which are common intestinal infections. These can be treated by antibiotics.

Choosing Your Veterinarian

Along with you and your breeder, your veterinarian is vital to your Cocker Spaniel's health. Veterinarians vary in their expertise and experience. You want a knowledgeable and experienced veterinarian, ideally one who is very familiar with Cockers and the problems they may encounter. The more your vet knows about Cockers, the more reliable the diagnoses and effective the recommended treatments will be.

If you are close enough to your breeder, consider using the same veterinarian. If you are farther away, your breeder may be able to help by contacting other Cocker Spaniel owners to locate the better veterinarians in your area.

When possible, find your veterinarian before getting your Cocker. Make an appointment and visit with each vet you are considering. Discuss how to keep your Cocker Spaniel healthy and what problems you should look for. Ask how they handle emergencies. Most vets do not handle their own emergencies if there is an emergency clinic nearby.

COCKER CLUE

Your observations are the first line of defense in maintaining your Cocker's health. It is up to you to recognize what is normal for your dog. Check him regularly for any changes in body or behavior. Any abnormality may warrant a call to your veterinarian.

- *Eating more or less than normal.*
- *Drinking more or less than normal.*
- *Differences with urinating.*
- *Changes in stool, diarrhea.*
- *Vomiting or straining to vomit.*
- *Changes in posture. Stiff, uncoordinated, trembling.*
- *Limping.*
- *Changes in energy level. More active, weak, lethargic.*
- *Changes in behavior. More irritable, withdrawn, needy.*
- *Changes in breathing. More labored, excessive panting.*
- *Lumps, bumps, or abrasions.*
- *Changes in coat—dry, oily, breaking, excessive shedding.*
- *Asymmetry.*
- *Indications of tenderness, soreness, or pain.*
- *Discharge from ears, nose, mouth, eyes, vulva, penis, or anus.*
- *Changes in mouth. Sore, loose, or broken teeth, changes in gums.*
- *For males, changes in size or texture of testicles.*
- *Weight change.*
- *Coughing or gagging.*
- *Fever. Normal temperature is 101–102°F.*
- *Abnormal odor.*
- *Repeated scratching or licking.*

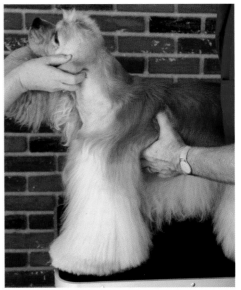

Check your Cocker weekly and advise your veterinarian of any irregularities that you find.

Remember that the best veterinarian for you and your Cocker may not be the one nearest to you.

Exercise and Condition

Your Cocker Spaniel is a sporting dog, temperamentally and physically suited to work in the fields finding and retrieving birds. He will be happiest if exercise is a part of each day, both to condition his body and mind and also to expend his energy. Well-exercised, he will be a calmer, more relaxed home companion.

If he is not in an enclosed, fenced area and doesn't yet reliably come when called,

Neighborhood walks can be a family affair.

keep him on lead. Off-lead exercise should be limited to fenced areas. There is no point is risking his life.

Long walks are great for Cockers (and you, too), but don't take puppies for lengthy hikes. Puppies need primarily free exercise where they can stop the split second they want to. Longer walks don't allow them to stop this way, unless you are willing to carry your puppy home.

Be aware of your walking surface. Concrete and asphalt can be hard on a dog's feet. Further, they are hot on hot days and can add to your dog's discomfort. Ice and snow can be slippery; your dog is barefoot on that frigid surface. If the weather is bad, consider exercise inside. Play games of fetch and hide-and-seek indoors.

If the exercise is strenuous or the weather is warm, remember to bring water along for your Cocker to drink. Dogs don't have

an efficient cooling system; they perspire only through the pads of their feet. Cooling water is important.

Spaying and Neutering

Your Cocker must remain intact if you plan to show him in conformation dog shows and later to breed him. For all other activities, spaying and neutering are advisable.

In many dog sports, a female in season is prohibited from attending. Intact males may be feisty with other dogs. They are also more likely to lift their leg to urinate and mark territory, and may do so in the house. Females come into season twice a year, at which time they have a vaginal discharge. Her odor will attract wandering males. If you have an intact male, you will have to keep them separated at this time. Intact males are always on the alert for a female and may run off in search of love.

Some are advising early neutering, probably to ensure that pet owners actually do it. Neutering after the Cocker is a year old is preferable. This allows him to have all his hormones to contribute to and help control his maturation.

Spaying females avoids serious uterine infections and if done before her first heat cycle, reduces the risk of mammary cancer by 95 percent. Neutered males won't get testicular cancer and are less likely to have prostate problems. There is the risk of surgery and anesthesia to consider, but most feel the benefits of having a neutered dog outweigh the risks.

8 Grooming

Owning a Cocker Spaniel means making a commitment to grooming. Some of the grooming tasks are done with all breeds, but the Cocker's crowning glory involves more coat care than other breeds. This is true regardless of the hairstyle you choose, although keeping it long will entail more time. Shorter haircuts still require regular trimming to keep the hair tidy and neat.

Groomers

You can do your own grooming if you have the time, inclination, and adequate talent. You can learn from your breeder, from books and videos, or even from schools. You will need more equipment, especially tools used for hair care, which will cost more money. You can practice and learn on your puppy. Most mistakes will correct themselves as the coat grows and you learn how to groom. You might have someone else trim your Cocker first so you can follow the pattern.

Alternatively, you can consider a professional groomer. It is more expensive on an on-going basis, as a Cocker needs grooming at least every six weeks. If your Cocker's coat tends to mat or tangle easily, grooming once every four weeks is better.

If you opt for a professional groomer, it is preferable to find one before getting your dog. Recommendations from other Cocker owners will be helpful. Visit and talk to the groomer before making your selection. Ask if he is familiar with Cockers. If he feels that Cockers are a snappy, temperamental breed, and may have been bitten, you might look for someone else. Some states have groomers or grooming shops licensed or certified. If your area has any requirements, make sure they are fulfilled. Ask if you can watch them groom other dogs; the dogs should be happy and comfortable, safely and gently handled.

Determine if the professional groomer is skilled in the coat care you need. If you are going to show your dog, make sure the groomer is experienced in show grooming; most are not. For instance, the back coat on a show Cocker is never clippered, while it usually is on a pet with a shorter haircut. Your breeder or a professional handler can help with show grooming.

If at all possible, take a photo of a dog with trim style you want the groomer to produce with your dog. Terminology isn't always consistent, and you and the groomer may have different interpretations of terms like "puppy cut."

Accustom your puppy to going to a groomer when she is very young, even though she won't have much coat yet. You should be able to watch your puppy being groomed, but be aware that some dogs misbehave more when the owner is present.

Equipment

How much equipment you get will depend on whether you groom your dog entirely yourself or use the services of a groomer. Get good quality products and equipment. The less expensive ones won't work well, and grooming will be more difficult.

Your Cocker will need regular brushing, even if you use a groomer. A grooming table for your puppy to stand on while you work will make the task easier. It needs a non-slip surface and must be sturdy. Some tables have adjustable legs, which allow you to work standing up or sitting down. It is also easier to do other grooming chores, such as teeth and ear care and nail clipping, with the dog on a grooming table. A grooming table with an arm has a loop that goes around the puppy's neck like a collar to help hold her in place. Never leave your Cocker unattended on the table even for a second. She may jump off and, if the loop is around her neck, hang herself.

A pin brush and a medium steel-toothed comb are basic for brushing and combing a Cocker. A slicker brush and mat rake are used to work out tangles and mats. Flea combs with close-together teeth can help you find those parasites in the coat. A stripping knife is used to groom the back coat on show Cockers, removing the undercoat so that the remaining hairs lie flat.

If you will be trimming your Cocker's coat, you will need clippers made for dogs. Some come with easily changed blades identified by number. The higher the number, the closer the blade will cut. Scissors are also used for trimming, including thinning shears.

If you will cut your dog's nails, get nail clippers. Also get styptic powder in case you cut a nail too close. To bathe your Cocker, you will need shampoo and cream rinse. You may invest in a blow-dryer meant for dogs to help dry the coat.

Training for Grooming

Your Cocker has probably been groomed two or three times before arriving at your home, including clipping, nail care, and brushing. Ask your breeder what he has done so far.

Continue training your Cocker for grooming when you get her. Put a towel on a grooming table for comfort. If you don't have a grooming table, a rubber mat on the counter or a sturdy table will do.

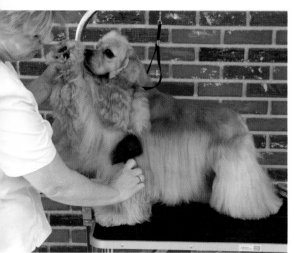

Much coat grooming is done with your Cocker on a grooming table, including brushing thoroughly under the forelegs to avoid mats.

Keep the sessions very short, a few minutes to start.

Stand her on the table facing to your right or left. Tell her "Stay." Stoke her back or gently hold her in place so she cannot walk around. Wait for a count of ten, then tell her "Good Girl!" and give her a tiny treat and take her off the table. Repeat the exercise several times each day.

As she learns to stand on the table, brush her coat while she is standing. Again, start with short sessions, then increase the time. Give her a treat each time for cooperating.

As she is more comfortable on the table, handle her gently all over. Lift her ears and pretend to clean with a cotton ball. Lift her lips and look at her teeth. Feel her all over, examining, rather than petting. Lift each foot and touch her nails. Give her an extra treat for letting you play with her feet.

Also teach her to lie on her side for brushing. Place her on her side. Hold her there by stroking gently. Give her a treat. Turn her over and repeat. Brush her gently.

Teach her about the hair-dryer. Let her see it without it being turned on. When she has investigated it, turn it on, but not blowing on her. Then let it blow on her feet and legs. Have it on low speed and low heat initially and hold it farther away until she becomes comfortable with it. Remember to treat her with each step.

Continue the exercises when doing very short actual grooming sessions. Give her a treat for each ear you clean, for each nail you trim, and for letting you brush her teeth. These will necessarily be tiny treats, or she will be getting too much extra food.

Never leave her unattended on a table or counter. Teach your pup where the edge is. Some do this by standing the Cocker with her rear feet very near an edge. Then holding the puppy's rear so that she doesn't actually fall, hang the puppy's rear end off the edge so that she hasn't a firm footing. Also, when standing securely on the table and being held, let her look over the edge.

Your veterinarian and whoever does her grooming will be very happy to have a dog that is comfortable and happy to be handled.

Ear Care

Thanks to their pendulous ears, Cockers tend to have more ear problems and infections than breeds with erect ears. Regular grooming and cleaning can mitigate against problems. Avoid getting water in the ear canal. Damp ears can result in both bacterial and yeast infections, both require a veterinarian's attention.

Clean the ear opening with a cotton ball dampened with hydrogen peroxide, alcohol, or canine ear cleaner. Swab clean

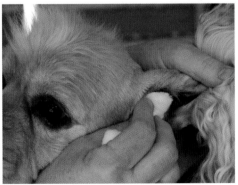

Regular ear cleaning helps avoid ear problems.

all the areas you can reach. Cotton swabs can clean in the grooves.

Some dogs seem to produce more wax in their ears than others and need to be cleaned more often. Check your Cocker's ears several times a week. If she is scratching or rubbing her ears or if you notice redness, she may have an infection. A bad smell may be a yeast infection. Have your veterinarian examine her.

The drooping ears of the Cocker can be kept cleaner with a snood. But don't leave the snoods on for extended times. They can exacerbate the incidence of infections by keeping light and air from the ears.

Dental Care

For healthy teeth and sweeter breath, take regular care of your Cocker's teeth. A soft toothbrush and doggy toothpaste are recommended. Your finger wrapped with a washcloth can substitute for the toothbrush. Safe, raw bones can help keep plaque under control. Check her mouth

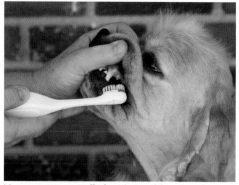

You can use a small electric toothbrush on your Cocker's teeth.

Hold the coat hair away from the nail when clipping the nail.

regularly for loose teeth, pale gums, growths—anything out of the usual. During your Cocker's annual exam, your veterinarian should check to see if she needs her teeth professionally cleaned, which is done under anesthesia.

Nail Care

It is easy for a coated dog's nails to get too long, for the hair covers the nails. But you should never hear the nails clicking on the floor. Nails that are left too long can result in flat feet and splayed toes. Further, the quick, the blood vessel that grows in the nail, will also grow further down into long nails, making it harder to clip the nails short. Long nails can get caught in carpet loops and pulled out. It is important for the health of your Cocker's feet to keep her nails short. Plan on trimming them at least once a month or more frequently.

You can use a clipper to trim nails. The clipper may be either guillotine or scissor style, your preference. After bathtime is a

A thorough brushing is done with your Cocker lying on her side on the grooming table.

good time to clip nails, when they are soft from the water.

Be careful not to cut into the quick. If your dog has light-colored or white nails, you can see the quick, which looks pink. With black nails, the best you can do is to look underneath the nail to see what part is just nail and where the "meat" extends to.

Coat Care

Even if you use a professional groomer to trim your Cocker, you will need to brush her and bathe her regularly. A long show coat will take even more care. The desired coat texture is silky and is flat or slightly wavy. This coat will shed dirt and debris better. If your Cocker has a curly or cottony coat, it will need more care.

Brushing

Thorough brushing is critical to Cocker coat care regardless of the length of the coat. Shorter coats, those with good texture, and dogs that don't get dirt in their hair can probably be brushed and combed twice a week. An every-other-day schedule is better. Time invested in brushing your Cocker means less time spent removing hair from your clothes and furniture, chasing dog-hair dust bunnies, and removing mats.

First, spray the coat with water mixed with a small amount of coat conditioner. Start from the bottom of the legs and work upward. Brush the coat down in the direction of the growth. Hold the coat above out of the way so that you can brush down to the skin. After you finish a section, brush the next narrow section of coat above. Continue until you have brushed all the coat. Be sure you get into the underarms behind the elbows, the underside of the dog, and the portions around the genitals, anus, and ears.

After brushing the entire coat, go through it again with a steel comb. Make sure there is not one tangle, mat, or bit of matter left in the coat to cause problems later.

COCKER CLUE

You will have to deal with mats in your Cocker's coat at some point. The sooner one is removed, the easier.

- *Saturate mat with detangling lotion.*
- *Let sit for five to ten minutes.*
- *Use your fingers initially to pull the mat apart in several directions.*
- *Use the end of a metal comb to separate hairs at the edge and pick apart into smaller mats.*
- *Continue with slicker brush on the smaller mats.*
- *Pin the adjacent hair that isn't involved away from the mat, so it won't get in your way.*
- *Don't stress or hurt the dog when dematting.*
- *Never bathe a dog that has any mats, because water tightens the mats and makes them harder to remove.*
- *If the mat cannot be worked out and/or is too close to the skin, it may have to be cut out. If close to the skin, this is better done by an experienced groomer. If you plan to cut out a mat, put a comb between the mat and the dog's skin before you start cutting to avoid accidentally cutting your dog.*

Bathing

Schedule a bath for your Cocker once a week or so. Brush your dog thoroughly before getting her wet. Some recommend putting cotton in the ears to keep them dry; this will work as long as the cotton doesn't get soaked. Others also put some ophthalmic ointment in the eyes to protect them.

Wet the dog completely with tepid water. The more coat, the harder it will be to soak through to the skin. A spray attachment is most useful in wetting the coat and is even more critical when rinsing. Use a rubber mat in the sink or tub to keep her from slipping. Have the drain open so your puppy won't be standing in dirty water.

There are many good shampoos available formulated for dogs. A protein-based shampoo should strengthen the hair. Tearless shampoo is good around the head and face. Some wash a dog's face and feet with a washcloth. Make sure you work the shampoo into the coat and down to the skin. After washing, rinse the coat and rinse again. Run your hands over all the coat, and if you feel anything slick, rinse some more.

After the rinse, apply cream rinse to help your Cocker's coat be more manageable and reduce tangles. Use a cream rinse or conditioner formulated for canines. Some are left in, others are rinsed out. Follow the directions.

After wiping as much water as possible off in the tub, wrap your Cocker in a large, thick towel to absorb more water. Squeeze, don't rub, for that can cause tangles. Comb the wet hair to make sure there are no tangles.

If your Cocker has a long coat, you can use a blow-dryer to accelerate drying. This is especially important when the weather is cooler. Use a dog blow-dryer that blows with more force but less heat than human dryers, which are too hot for dogs. If you do much grooming, a stand to hold the dryer is a big help. Brush the coat while drying it.

Don't brush your Cocker's wet coat without drying it at the same time. If you don't have a grooming stand and if you are dexterous, you can tuck a hand-held dryer under your arm or chin and aimed at your dog. Brush in the direction the air is blowing. This way you will get down to the skin with both brushing and drying.

Light-colored and parti-colored Cockers with white legs will show dirt more often. Touch-up bathing of legs and feet may be needed. Self-rinse and waterless shampoos can be used if you don't want to use water.

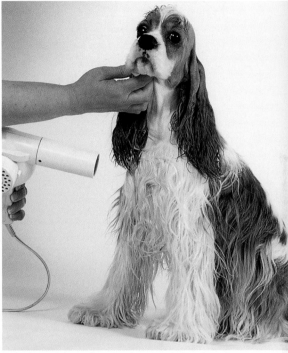

To help avoid tangles, simultaneously brush and blow-dry your Cocker's coat after a bath.

Coat Trimming

The trim on your Cocker is your decision, possibly based on the activities in which you plan to participate. Whether you do it yourself or use a professional, trimming should be done every four to six weeks, depending on the style and the quality of the coat.

If you choose the easiest pet coat for your Cocker, your can trim her short all over with a #4, #5, or #7 blade, depending on the length of hair that you want.

If you hunt or compete in field trials, leave at least one and a half to two inches on your Cocker's legs and abdomen to protect her from the underbrush. Do not keep your dog in a long coat if she is doing any water work. It will become soaked and heavy, making it very hard to swim dragging the extra weight. Cockers have drowned because they had too much coat to work in water.

Whatever her haircut, make sure you also trim the hair that grows between the pads of her feet even with the pad. Trim around the anus with scissors.

Dogs not being shown may trim the coat closer in areas more likely to develop mats, such as around and under the elbows.

COCKER CLUE

Use sprays to help cool and lubricate the clipper blade. If it becomes too hot, it can burn when it touches the dog's skin. Disinfectants are available to keep your tools, including the blades, sterile.

Clipper burn happens when the blade gets too hot. It can cause irritation or a rash, and the dog may scratch until there is an open sore. Wash the area and treat with an antibiotic cream. Consider leaving that area coat a bit longer in the future.

Keeping blades in the refrigerator will keep them cool. Clipper sensitive areas first, when the clipper is fresh and cool.

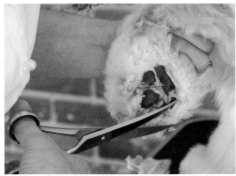

For safety as well as appearance, trim the hair that grows between and around the pads.

Show Coat

If you will show your Cocker, she will have to keep her coat long. Each part of the dog is trimmed separately. Hair is typically short on the head, a bit longer but not long on the back, longer on the sides, legs, and abdomen. The clippers are used on the head, ears, neck, and shoulders, but not on the body. Generally you should clip in the direction that the hair grows.

The muzzle is clipped short with a #10 blade. This includes the chin and the cheeks. Stretch the upper lips to trim them more easily, and be careful under the eyes.

With the same blade, trim the top third of the ear, lifting the clipper as you reach the skull so you don't leave a ridge. Clip the inside of the ear leather, too, to the same point as done on the outer. Trim the hair hanging from the ears in a slightly rounded shape.

Continue with the clipper to trim the underside of the neck to a "V" shape two inches above the prosternum. Use a #8½ or #7 blade on the sides and back of the

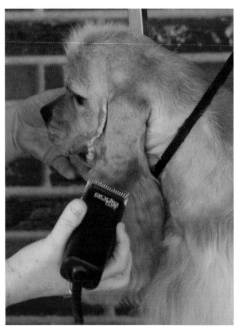

It takes practice to do a good job trimming a Cocker.

Trim your Cocker's coat as the arrows indicate.

neck where the coat should be longer. The neck hair should flow smoothly into the back hair with no perceptible line.

Trim the back half of the skull, going with the hair. The front half of the skull and brows are trimmed with thinning sheers. It is left long enough to emphasize a deep stop and domed skull. Blend the hairs when trimming so that there isn't an abrupt line. The goal is to emphasize the Cocker's characteristic soft, warm expression.

Be careful and conservative with thinning shears, for it is easy to take off too much or in the wrong place. Thin the coat lying underneath, not the surface guard hairs. Trim the undercoat that is making the upper coat not lie flat. Snip once (rather than multiple times) with the thinning shears, and then brush out the hair removed, and see what it looks like. Repeat until the desired look is achieved.

Remember that it takes a long time for a coat to grow back.

The coat on the back should lie flat. This usually involves stripping it with a stripping knife to remove the undercoat. The remaining coat hanging from the lower part of the body is trimmed level. You can use thinning shears to blend the back coat with the longer coat on the sides. Trim the coat on the tail. Never use clippers on the back coat.

The coat on the front, sides, and the feather on the legs is left untrimmed. Feet are trimmed to a round shape. The coat is beveled at the foot by holding the scissors at an angle so that the outside hairs on the leg are trimmed slightly shorter than those nearest the leg.

From start to finish, including bathing, drying, and trimming, it can take two hours or more to prepare a Cocker Spaniel in full show coat for the show ring.

Trim the head in the direction of the arrows.

9 *Basic Training*

Cocker Spaniels don't like repetition and are easily bored. Keep your training sessions short and fun. Cockers are very social creatures. Distractions call to them, and focusing on you to the exclusion of all else does not come naturally. To get the most out of training, make certain that your Cocker has thoroughly learned *attention* (see Chapter 4). When his attention is on you, he can better understand what you are teaching.

Some Cockers learn very quickly, while others are slower to learn. It is best not to compare your puppy to others of the same age. Dogs mature at different rates, and males tend to mature later than females.

Reward your Cocker multiple times a day for good behavior to reinforce the behaviors you want. Give him a treat when he comes to you, when he lies quietly, when he obeys whatever command you are working on, when he retrieves a toy, when he lets you examine him all over, or when he cooperates with grooming. There should be many opportunities each day to tell him what a good boy he is.

Equipment

You'll need a six-foot lead for basic training, although when you are in a confined area at home with few distractions, you can coax your puppy to do what you want off-lead. Single-ply nylon is comfortable to hold and light in weight. Collar preference varies. Some use a metal choke collar when training; others prefer buckle or quick-clip collars.

Have treats and toys to lure your Cocker into the behavior you want. Many trainers use string cheese, which can be pinched into tiny pieces to treat, carried in your pocket, or even put in your mouth. Beef jerky or pressed meats work too, as does white-meat chicken, which is less oily than dark meat. Try different treats to see for which your dog will work best. He will learn faster when you lure him than if you touch or push him into the behavior or position you want.

Sit

Hold a treat slightly above your Cocker's nose and head so that he has to look up to see and focus on it. Move it back toward his ears so he looks up. Don't hold it so high that he will jump for it. Hold it so he cannot take it from your fingers. As he looks up, his bottom will lower toward the floor. As it lowers, say "Good Boy!" and give him a treat.

Repeat, but give the treat when his bottom is lowered closer to the floor. Encourage him with your voice and by holding the treat in such a way that he will move into the position you want. Some dogs may back up, and you might have to back them up against a wall or piece of furniture before their rears get lower. Repeat again, each time rewarding further progress towards sitting. He will figure out that he can get the goody by putting his butt on the floor.

Note that we haven't said "*Sit!*" yet, because he doesn't know what the word means. After you have the behavior being done reliably for the lure, you can add the command. Continue using the treat at the same time as giving the command. Say "*Sit!*" as a command, assertively, not as a request. Tone of voice is more meaningful to your Cocker than the word.

When using the command, say it once and still using the lure, wait for your Cocker to do it. He'll get the concept: he doesn't get the treat until his fanny is on the floor. Don't keep repeating the command. That's nagging and background noise. Why should he *sit* when he knows that you're going to say it again?

Don't repeat the command when the dog is already sitting. It will confuse him. *Sit* means putting his bottom on the ground, an action that he cannot do when he is already sitting. Dogs don't equate an action with a position.

As you present the treat, start using the hand signal that will be the equivalent of the *sit* command. Hold the treat in your palm with your thumb, keeping your hand open, with your arm at your side. Lift your arm from the elbow, palm up, towards your Cocker. You'll be giving three messages with the same request—the treat, the *sit* verbal command, and the *sit* hand signal. When he knows them, vary the

Be creative in building the arsenal that you will use to encourage your Cocker to learn.

game; sometimes use the word, sometimes the hand signal. Dogs alert to movement. Your Cocker may respond faster to the hand signal.

Location

Dogs are context learners. If you teach him *sit* when you are in the family room, he knows sit-in-the-family-room. Your dog won't necessarily generalize that *Sit!* should also be done in the kitchen, the patio, and the driveway. So make sure you practice your sits in as many different locations and situations as you can, until he does generalize the command based on the many experiences.

He also knows *sit* when *you* say it. When he reliably sits for you, have other family members instruct him to *sit,* and remember to have them include the treat.

Down

Instructing your dog to lie down is logically the next step from *sit*. The command is "*Down!*," not "*Lie down.*" Your puppy can learn a word easier than a phrase. With your Cocker in a sitting position, hold a treat in front of your dog's nose and move it down at an angle towards the floor. As his nose, and head, follows the treat to the ground, his elbows should get to the ground, too. If his rear pops up, start over. When his elbows touch the ground, give him the treat and praise.

If he doesn't catch on quickly, start by rewarding his downward movement. Then on each successive try, reward him for being lower than before. Pretty soon, he'll be all the way down.

When he can be reliably lured down, attach the command, "*Down!*" just as you did with *sit*. Further, the hand and arm motion of taking the treat from a higher position to a lower position is similar to the hand signal for *down*. Start with your arm extended straight up, and bring it down as you were bringing the treat down. Use them all together: the verbal "*Down*," the treat, and the hand signal.

Come

The *come* or recall is probably the most important of all commands to teach your Cocker. Start, even informally, when he is a young puppy. Make it fun; it must always be wonderful for your puppy to come when you call.

Crouch down with a treat, call his name and say, "*Come!*" Use an enthusiastic high-

Leave your Cocker's lead on when you train in an unsecured area.

It sounds quite different to him coming from other people.

Practice the *sit* command before giving your Cocker anything he wants. Have him *sit* for his meal, *sit* for you to open the door, *sit* before going for a walk, *sit* for having a ball thrown, *sit* for a toy. Each thing he wants and gets—the meal, the opened door, the walk—he earns by sitting on request. In a day you can easily get a dozen practices this way.

When your Cocker is reliably sitting on command from a standing position, practice having him *sit* from the *down* position. It is a totally different action for him to learn, so start from the beginning, and lure him into the *sit* position when he is lying down. Use the command, hand signal, and lots of praise.

COCKER CLUES
- *Never train when you are angry or in a bad mood.*
- *Never correct a dog for not doing something he hasn't yet learned.*
- *Train in the middle of playtime and make training a part of play.*
- *After a command has been learned, proof it with distractions.*
- *Progress gradually in small steps to get the most success.*

Calling your dog to you should never result in something your dog doesn't like. Don't call him to bathe, clip nails, to crate, or give pills. In those instances, go get him. Don't put an end to playtime when you call him either. Call him, then let him go back to playing multiple times, so he doesn't equate coming to you as the end of the fun. To do otherwise will teach him not to *come*.

Heel

pitched voice to encourage him. When he comes, praise and pet him and give him a treat or a toy. Several times a day when he isn't paying attention, call your Cocker to you and give him a treat. Don't give treats when he comes of his own volition. He gets credit and a reward only when he does it when you say to.

Practice in lots of different places, all enclosed, until your dog is totally reliable. Use a long line (a lead about sixteen feet long) in your practices in unfenced places.

As your Cocker becomes more reliable with his recall, add more distractions. It isn't enough to come in your backyard when nothing else is going on. Your dog must also come when you call even when he is tempted otherwise. Add distractions a little at a time, beginning with mild ones that are at a distance and therefore less intense. Gradually increase the strength or reduce the distance of the distraction. Don't increase the intensity or reduce the distance at the same time. When you increase the temptation of the distraction, you may want to initially start it farther away.

Heeling officially has your Cocker walking at your left side with his head by your leg. Most of the time, you'll be pleased if your dog walks with you without pulling. But other times you will want him to stay closer and more under control.

Start by encouraging your puppy to follow you with a treat, a toy, clapping your hands, and with your voice. Entice him to be on your left side as you walk forward by keeping the treat-filled hand or toy by your left leg. This is where you want his head to be. Keep walking and lure him to continue walking next to your leg by giving a tiny treat often. (This requires some coordination on your part so that you don't fall down or walk into anything.)

As he gets the concept, offer the treats less often. When he is also comfortable with the lead, continue the process with the lead on. Keep the lead on whenever practicing in an unfenced area.

When he's good at walking at heel position, change your speed—walk fast then walk slowly. Lure your dog to adjust his speed to yours. Practice turning right and left, luring him into the turns with a treat.

Teaching your dog to *heel* will come in handy during most of the activities you share with your Cocker.

Do an about turn, turning to walk in the opposite direction. Practice walking with your Cocker in curved, circular paths. When you circle left, he'll be on the inside of the turn and will have to slow down. When you circle right, he will be on the outside of the turn and will have to speed up to stay next to you.

Stop, and he should stop with you. Tell him *sit* when you stop—unless you plan to show your Cocker. Dogs don't *sit* in the show ring, so don't train for automatic *sits* with show dogs.

Each time you start walking, say "*Heel!*" While learning, repeat the command, associating the word with the behavior. As he understands the behavior, you can reduce the frequency of the lures and treats, so that he just gets a treat periodically.

Stay

Stay is different from your Cocker's point of view, for you are asking him not to do something, to not move. The secret is to progress in tiny increments. Tell your dog to sit. Put your palm in front of his muzzle, and say, "*Stay!*" Count to five, tell him, "*Okay*" (or your release word) and what a good boy he is, and give him a treat. If he anticipates and breaks the *stay*, then no treat.

Don't say your puppy's name with the *stay* command. His name with a command is usually a call to action, and with *stay* you want inaction.

When he can *stay* for a short count, have him *stay* for a count of 10, then 15, then 20. When he can do it reliably by your side, tell him to "*Stay!*" and step in front of him. You've changed the setup, so go

The hand signal reinforces the verbal command to "stay."

back to the shorter time. When he can *stay* with you in front, give the *stay* command and take one step away. Each time you change your location or distance or your Cocker's position, step back with shorter *stays*. At the end of each *stay*, release him with *"Okay,"* or whatever release word you have chosen.

After your Cocker has mastered staying in a sitting position, have him learn to *stay* in the *down* position. This is especially useful to use when you have company and you want to include your dog, but lying down and out of the way. It also demonstrates good manners when you visit a sidewalk cafe that welcomes canine companions.

Trainers

Ideally you will train your Cocker yourself. But some folks opt to have a professional trainer train their dog. If you choose this route, make certain that you are trained as well. You want your dog to work for you as well as the trainer.

Professional in-home obedience training is an expensive option. The first challenge is finding a good trainer. You want one with Cocker experience. You can start with referrals from friends, your veterinarian, your breeder, and from people with well-behaved dogs.

Call and interview the instructors on their experience and accomplishments, training techniques, and philosophies. A good trainer emphasizes positive reinforcement with minimum corrections. Ask about the dogs they have personally trained and the types they have worked with. Ask for their opinions of Cockers, their tempera-

ment and learning styles. Inquire about affiliation with professional associations, such as the National Association of Dog Obedience Instructors (NADOI), Pet Dog Trainers (APDT), and International Association of Canine Professionals (IACP).

There are several benefits to in-home private training. Primarily, private training can be tailored to your dog with more one-on-one attention and instruction. The entire family can be included in the training sessions, targeting any issues or problems that your dog may have. Further, there is often more flexibility in scheduling private sessions.

Classes

Group classes are a less expensive option to train your dog. Some of the better ones are offered by dog obedience clubs. They are taught by club members who have earned obedience titles with their dogs. These instructors train as a hobby and are less likely to be licensed professionals than those whose vocation is dog training. Some pet stores also offer classes, but these tend to be more expensive. More expensive still are private obedience schools.

Visit the classes you are considering and observe the training process. Not all trainers are the same; there are different styles and techniques. Many trainers have more experience and expertise with one type of dog. Look for a trainer experienced with Cockers.

Group classes have many benefits. Your Cocker learns to train and work in the company of other dogs. He is also in a different place with other distractions. You get the benefits of an expert trainer at a

COCKER CLUE

Training off-lead in your own home and enclosed yard with your dog under control is fine. Too many people are tempted to try a dog off-lead too soon in a less controled or confined area. Puppies and adolescents are often not mature enough to handle the distractions and will be curious and run off. Wait until the training is strongly reliable on lead before considering off-lead work.

and a four-month-old Great Dane may not be compatible.

The basic or beginning class is usually for dogs at least six months old. It introduces the dogs to the basic commands mentioned above. Some trainers offer advanced basic classes, which polish the performance on the basic commands. Clubs may offer special classes geared to a specific technique, such as clicker training, or preparation for passing a test, such as earning a Canine Good Citizen title.

An oddly-named advanced class is the novice class, which helps prepare people and their dogs for the novice obedience level competition. There will also be classes that help students learn exercises in open and utility. Rally classes, to prepare for rally competitions, are also popular.

Determine your goals before training. What do you want to do with your Cocker and what do you expect from him? A sound foundation of basic obedience commands is required for showing, hunting, competitions of obedience, agility, and rally, and to shape a pleasant, well-mannered member of your family.

reasonable price. You still must do your homework, practicing daily with your puppy at home.

There are multiple levels of obedience classes. The first is puppy kindergarten. These are primarily for socialization and an introduction to gentle, positive play training. Some puppy classes are divided by age and/or size, since a four-month-old Yorkie

10 *Dealing with Problems*

You aren't perfect; neither is your Cocker. Sometimes she will do things that you consider undesirable. That is your point of view, though, not your Cocker's. Many actions we don't like are quite natural and self-reinforcing for dogs.

Dogs, like people, do what works for them. Unlike people, they don't do things for spite or revenge. Try to see things from your Cocker's perspective as you try to modify the behavior. Understand why she is doing or not doing something—we are supposed to be the smarter species, after all.

There are choices in dealing with problem behavior. Different problems may have different solutions. If you can prevent trouble from happening in the first place, you are way ahead of the game. You can try to modify or correct the behavior, either yourself or with the help of a professional trainer. You can also manage, rather than eliminate the problem. This may be the choice for those situations that are difficult to correct or when you aren't willing to invest the time to address them.

Avoidance

An ounce of prevention is worth a pound of cure is emphatically true with dogs. If you can stop a habit from being formed by preventing the opportunity, you can avoid the problem in the first place.

Puppies and adolescents are curious and will investigate their surroundings. They try different behaviors, including jumping, chewing, digging, and barking, to see what works and what is fun. You are in charge of your Cocker's environment. Don't give her unsupervised access to situations in which she can get into trouble. Did she chew the couch? Keep her away from furniture when you aren't watching. Did she dig a hole in the garden? Don't leave her alone in the yard for longer periods in which she'll need to invent her own games.

Among your tools for avoidance are the crate, exercise pens, and baby gates. Keep your Cocker's environment limited as she learns the house rules and forms habits. Allow access to bones and toys, and other "allowed" play objects. As you give her more freedom, supervise so you can correct any behaviors you don't want.

It requires vigilance on your part to limit your Cocker's access to trouble. If the lid is up on the toilet, she may investigate the interesting pool of water. The open door to the bathroom lets her find toilet paper; she can grab the end and run down the hall, or chew it on the roll, creating toilet paper doilies. But remember, you let it happen.

If you decide not to allow your Cocker on the furniture, be sure to consistently enforce your decision.

Housetraining

Housetraining problems usually start with the owner. Make sure you have followed the instructions in Chapter 4 for using a crate, controlling your Cocker's access to places, getting her outside when she needs to go, scheduling food and water, and thoroughly cleaning up and disinfecting after accidents.

If you are doing everything right, maturity may be the issue. A puppy can "hold it" for about as many hours as its age in months. For example, a four-month-old puppy will need to urinate every four hours. Your Cocker may be five or six months old before she is housetrained.

Have a veterinarian check your Cocker for any problems that might be the cause. She may have a bladder or urinary infection, thyroid problems, or intestinal parasites. Some dogs drink too much water and have to urinate all the time. This can be resolved by giving her smaller amounts

COCKER CLUE
Prevent problems by providing your puppy with as much play and exercise as she can handle. In other words, tire her out. Run in the yard, taking turns chasing each other. Toss a ball and practice retrieving (your puppy should go get the ball, not you). A tired puppy is a good puppy. She won't be bored and looking for her own fun and games. Don't force the exercise, though. Puppies must be able to stop the second they want to. Since Cockers may have joint problems, exercise is better on soft surfaces such as grass or sand rather than concrete or asphalt.

of water several times a day rather than letting her drink all she wants.

If you catch her in the act, you can correct her verbally and whoosh her out to the place you want her to go. But if you don't catch her doing it, don't correct her, for she will have no idea why you are unhappy. It may even provoke submissive urination as she tries to appease your anger.

The correction should never involve hitting your Cocker. Make it verbal or you can use a noisemaker such as a shaker can with some pebbles or dried beans in it, to startle her.

Another option, if your home permits, is to install a doggy door giving her access to a safe place outside to go potty. Her crate must provide easy access to the doggy door for this to be effective.

Submissive Urination

Submissive urination is not a housetraining issue for it has different causes and different solutions. Some Cockers have a tendency to this problem. If it is caused by puppy excitability, it may be outgrown.

Dogs indicate their submission to authority by urinating. You will make the problem worse by correcting her or even leaning over her, for both are dominant

gestures to your Cocker. She will try to submit more, resulting in more dribbling. Do your best to not add to the intimidation. Ignore her; don't talk to her or even look at her. Head straight for the door and let her out. Go out with her, but pay no attention—no leaning over her, no touching at her. When she does pee, tell her calmly what a good girl she is, and give her a treat.

If the urination is due to excitement, your goal is to reduce the excitement. Again, ignoring your Cocker will be effective. Don't talk or look at her, both of which could make her more excited.

In both cases, try tossing bits of a really tasty treat away from you. The attention paid to the treats will take the focus off the fear or excitement, eliminating the need to urinate.

Your puppy will sniff the floor and may turn partially around before squatting. If you see this behavior, you have a few seconds to get her outside.

83

Barking

Cocker Spaniels will alarm bark to alert you to visitors or passers-by. Left alone in a yard, she may bark at presumed intruders, and eventually to entertain herself. Some dogs bark because they feel lonely and isolated. Your initial task is to identify why she is barking.

Teach your puppy how to be alone for shorter periods and then gradually increase the time; your Cocker can learn patience. Confine her in her crate with treat-filled toys and chew toys to entertain her, so she won't notice she's alone.

Leave the radio or television on for her. This will also cover minor noises that might worry her and start her barking. A good exercise session can tire her out, so when you leave, she may be ready for a nap.

Your Cocker may bark to let you know someone is approaching. This is an appropriate behavior for a subordinate member of the pack to do— she's barking to alert the leader. Thank her and tell her that's enough, that you will take charge from here. Have her *sit* and give her a treat for her efforts.

You can also teach her to bark, the idea being that a dog trained to bark on command is less likely to do so on her own. Get her to bark on the command "*Speak!*" by imitating a bark—unless she is in process of barking. When she barks, give her a treat.

If she's barking because you left her outside for too long, bring her in. You owe that to your neighbors. Don't leave her out so long. If you forget, and she barks, and you bring her in, she's training you to let her in on command. That's fine if this is the system you want.

Electronic bark collars are available that, when triggered by the vibration of barking, deliver a short stimulation message to stop. Another device emits a high-pitched tone until the barking stops. A variant of bark collars is available that uses citrus as a deterrent. When the dog barks with the collar on, a squirt of citrus is aimed at her nose.

The last resort, not recommended unless the alternative is giving up the dog, is debarking. It is done surgically under anesthesia. A cut is made in the tissue around the vocal chords. The dog still barks, but sounds like she has extreme laryngitis.

Chewing

Puppies chew. They begin teething between three to six months and use their teeth to investigate their world and entertain themselves. To form good habits give them appropriate things to chew. Crates, gates, and supervision, will help you avoid the problem. Proper chewing can also help keep teeth clean and gums healthy.

Appropriate items include large, uncooked bones, sterilized natural bones, and nylon or hard rubber chew toys. Cold carrots are soothing to sore gums. Rawhide, hooves, pigs ears, and small or cooked bones are not recommended because small bits are often swallowed. Be especially careful that your Cocker cannot chew off a piece that can be swallowed, and don't give her anything to chew that resembles something you don't want her to chew. She won't know the difference between old shoes and socks and new ones. If your Cocker is chewing things she shouldn't, you

There are a wide variety of dog toys currently on the market. Select the most appropriate chew toys for your Cocker, so she won't be tempted to chew on your things.

can spray them with a product designed to taste nasty and prevent chewing.

If you are dealing with an adult dog with ingrained chewing habits, your best option is to give her alternative chew bones and toys and spray the things she shouldn't chew. Manage the situation by keeping her from the items she wants to chew, but shouldn't.

Jumping

Cocker Spaniels love to jump on people. They want attention, they want to be involved in everything, and they love to greet guests. But this enthusiasm can be annoying.

Kneeing the dog or trying to step on her back toes won't work well to combat this. First, you must be very agile. Second, your Cocker will think it is part of the game she has engaged you in. Turning your back and ignoring her won't work either. She can jump on your back; it's a fun game for her. You can move into her, but to her it is just another step in the dance, and no reason for her to stop.

What does work is supplying an alternate behavior. Tell her to *sit* or *down* and give her a treat. Give her attention for doing what *you* want, rather than what *she* wants.

If you reward your Cocker with petting and attention when she jumps on you, or allow jumping when you have old clothes on, she will continue to jump, even when you are all dressed up.

Another option is to make jumping unpleasant for her. When she jumps up, grab her front paws, one in each of your hands, and hold them. She won't like her paws being "trapped," and will try to pull away. Keep holding. If she tries to mouth your hands, move them away, but don't let go. Hold her paws and keep her standing for at least 30 seconds, up to one minute. This spoils her game. It may take a couple of tries, but pretty quickly she will jump, but not close enough for you to grab her paws. You'll not trick her again!

Digging

Dogs dig. It's fun, it creates nice cool dirt to lie on, it provides a tunnel under a fence, or is part of chasing a critter hiding underground. So we are at cross-purposes trying to get dogs not to dig.

If you can, provide a place in your yard where your dogs are allowed to dig. A sandbox is one option. Under a tree has advantages, since the roots and such will limit the progress. It may not be good for the tree, though.

If she's still digging where you don't want her to, put her stool in the holes. Dogs won't normally dig in feces. She may, of course, just dig another hole.

Management includes supervision and avoidance. Don't give her extensive alone time in the yard. Accompany her to the yard when she goes to exercise or play. If she can't be supervised, keep her in the house or on an enclosed patio where she cannot dig.

Aggression

Aggression is a very large topic, beyond the scope of this chapter. A few considerations will be mentioned. For serious problems, please consult a professional trainer.

Aggression needs to be identified properly to be handled properly. Aggression towards people is different from aggression towards dogs or other animals. It may be dominance based, but more likely it is fear based; each is handled differently. More

While a puppy looks cute in a basket, a Cocker should never be a surprise gift for anyone.

problems occur with poorly-bred dogs and with dogs that have suffered abuse. Fortunately, poor temperament is atypical of well-bred and well-cared-for Cockers.

Food and inadequate exercise can have negative effects on a dog's temperament. High protein food has been correlated to more aggressive behavior; check the dog food label, and consider a lower protein version. A well-exercised, tired, but happy, dog is less stressed and has less energy to be aggressive. This is a good reason to make sure your Cocker gets lots of exercise.

Children can be extremely annoying to a dog, and some Cockers have less tolerance for aggravation than others. When the dog is being harassed and cannot escape, she may snap in response. Children must be taught how to handle and respect a dog. No tail pulling, no ear pulling, no teasing. A responsible adult should actively supervise the time children spend with your Cocker; never leave a young child alone with your dog.

Types of Aggression

Some dogs are aggressive because it works and they've assumed leadership of the pack. Practice leadership behavior yourself, described in Chapter 5, to reinforce your position as head of your pack. Your dog will be happier when you take responsibility.

Some dogs have a strong prey drive and are aggressive to smaller animals—especially ones they don't live with. Some Cockers may have had bad experiences with other dogs and may respond with aggression that is fear-based and defensive.

Strong corrections don't help fear-based aggression. You can improve the situation with conditioning through attention and rewards. If your dog is afraid and aggressive with other dogs, begin by making sure you have your dog well trained with *attention*. Introduce another dog at a distance, barely within your Cocker's notice. When she notices the other dog, tell her, "*Watch me!*" and offer treats. Gradually, have the other dog come closer. Each time your dog notices the other dog, grab her attention, and reward her. With sufficient practice, the other dog will become associated with the *watch me* command. The goal is to change your dog's state of mind. Instead of excitement and arousal, the sight of another dog will prompt your Cocker to look at you, be happy, and get a treat.

Management may be an option in dealing with aggression. Keep your dog away from situations that provoke the misbehavior, such as other people's children or other dogs. Avoidance may not be the most elegant solution, but it is a way to manage a difficult problem.

Resource Guarding

The pack leader has priority access to limited and valued resources. Some dogs feel strongly about protecting what they feel is theirs, be it food, bones, or toys. Two behaviors can help with this problem.

Again, reinforce your leadership of the pack. You are in charge of food, doors, walks, balls, and other toys. The more your Cocker recognizes your leadership, the less she will challenge you.

Don't make it a frontal challenge, pulling her toy away or using force to take something. This will only provoke more

Most Cockers will share their toys, but there are some that will want to keep the toys for themselves.

jealous guarding and may result in her snapping at or biting you.

You are smarter than she is. Make it worth her while to not guard by offering her something better when you take what she has. Start this when she is a puppy. Toss her favorite toy to her with one hand while you sneak away the bone with the other. Regularly and early, reach into her food while she is eating to add some extra tasty morsels. She'll look forward to your fingers, for they are producing treats.

Shyness

Whether or not shyness is a problem depends on when you are dealing with it. You can make more progress faster with a young puppy than with an older dog who has a history of negative experiences.

Shyness with Cockers is much like with people. They lack confidence. They may be naturally reserved or be especially sensitive to noise, light, or change. You'll never turn an introvert into the life of the party, but you can bolster your puppy's confidence with substantial socialization.

Dogs are naturally sensitive to sounds, smells, and movement. Some dogs are more sensitive than others, and may be more extreme in their reactions. Desensitizing may help by providing your dog with extra exposure to stimulants, which in time will allow her to become more accustomed and comfortable in her environment.

Each day provide the opportunity for her to successfully experience something new. Don't push or force her. Don't rush her with big steps that may intimidate her. Let her investigate at her own speed. You should model quiet confidence; she'll look to you for an appropriate response. The more positive experiences she has, the more confidence she will have when meeting new ones.

Mouthing and Nipping

All puppies explore the world with their mouths. When they play with their littermates, they learn how hard is *too* hard when they nip and bite each other.

You need to teach your Cocker puppy to apply the same concept to people. She needs to learn bite inhibition. She will play with you and your family with her mouth, as she did with her siblings. When she puts her teeth on you, say "Ow!" sternly, and stop playing for a minute. You may also hold her muzzle and say "No!" Then ignore her. Cockers are social and want company. She will quickly learn that biting ends playtime. Progress to not allowing her to put her mouth on people at all.

When playing, don't wrestle with your puppy. Wrestling can cause arousal that can excite her so much that it escalates into using her mouth, much as she would when tussling with another dog.

Teach her to take food gently from your hand. Hold most of the treat in your palm with just a bit sticking out from the tips of your fingers. The only way she can get it is to gently nibble the bits that protrude. If she is too rough, take the treat away. She can only have it by being gentle.

Hyperactivity

Your Cocker is a sporting dog bred to hunt all day in the field. She still has that energy, even if she spends most of her time confined to your home. The best way to have a calmer Cocker is to make sure she has enough exercise. Schedule multiple play periods for your Cocker every day.

Puppies should have free exercise only. Putting a dog in a yard by herself isn't exercise. Another dog (if you have one) may get her playing. Children and Cockers can wear each other out. You can go out and play, too; the exercise will do you good.

> **COCKER CLUE**
>
> *Don't let your Cocker Spaniel have access to garbage; it can be dangerous to her. Cockers are food hounds—if some is good, more is better. One option is to keep your Cocker out of rooms that hold food garbage. Alternatively, you can contain the garbage so she cannot get to it. Some owners keep the garbage container in a cabinet under the sink. If that is not viable, get a garbage can with a secure lid that your Cocker cannot open. Those in which the edge of the lid is flush with the side of the can and opens with a foot pedal work well.*

Walks tailored to your Cocker's age are also good exercise. Go places, visit people, include socialization on your walks. You'll have a calmer Cocker when you return.

Watch her diet, too. Too many simple carbohydrates and too much protein can aggravate hyperactivity.

Separation Anxiety

Some Cockers get very stressed when left alone and may resort to barking or destructive behavior. There are several things you can try to relieve this situation—or even prevent it.

Again, exercise is key. If your Cocker is tired out from running and playing before you leave, she'll be less stressed, and more likely to sleep.

Condition her to be alone, by leaving her for very short periods—even just a few minutes—and returning. Make no fuss when you leave or return to increase her

Teach your Cocker to enjoy her alone time with toys and treats.

Running Off

Some Cockers will stay near you off lead, but many won't. Many are escape artists, eager to explore and follow their hearts and noses. Don't risk your Cocker's life by assuming that she won't run off. You must make sure it doesn't happen.

Make absolutely certain that your yard is securely fenced. There must be no gaps she could wiggle through and be gone. Make sure gates and doors are closed securely and cannot be opened by your clever dog. Outside in an unenclosed area, keep her on lead.

This is a family effort; everyone must cooperate to not give your Cocker the opportunity to get away. Adults and children cannot leave the doors open, even for a minute. A screen door can be pushed open, and your puppy will be gone, so make certain it is latched and, if necessary, locked. Service people must be advised to be extra careful. You don't want the song "Who Let The Dogs Out?" to refer to your Cocker.

Accidents do happen so have a backup plan. Teach her a reliable recall. Few dogs will respond when they are running away, but if she isn't running, and you call her to return, with treats, she'll likely come. Have her microchipped early and register with a national microchip service. Keep a lightweight tag on her collar that lists your phone number.

arousal. Repeat multiple times, gradually increasing the time you are gone. Do this with puppies whether they have a problem or not, to teach them patience.

Make being alone an extra pleasant time. Provide toys, hollow bones stuffed with peanut butter, extra treats hidden in toys, a carrot—things she especially likes. Save them for when she will be alone to make that time special.

11 *Obedience*

With the training you've done so far, you are well on your way to some obedience titles. These titles are earned by competing in AKC events, characterized as companion events. Unlike other "competitions," however, you don't need to defeat anyone to win. You are scored on how well your dog, and you, do the exercises, and if you two do well enough, you succeed.

Basic Training

Cockers generally are smart. But some want to know why, and won't always be willing to work just to please you. So provide your Cocker a reason to perform—a treat, a toy, extra petting and attention, whatever turns him on.

Stay focused on your dog during training. You taught him *attention*, and you'll need that attention when you train, so return the favor. Notice what he likes to do, and what he doesn't and evaluate which techniques work best with him, and which ones he doesn't respond to.

Some Cockers may get stressed more easily than others. Figure out what causes tension, and remove it or work elsewhere. Don't add to your Cocker's stress by making training a chore. If the stress is caused by his not mastering an exercise, practice more, adding distractions until he gains

confidence from success. Or add new lessons in smaller increments, so he can learn just a small new behavior.

Find a class that is teaching the exercises and the level you want to pursue. It isn't enough for your Cocker to work in and around your home. To compete, he will have to perform around different people and dogs and in other locations, and that is one of the many things you can get from class. Search for a class where the people and dogs are having a good time and making progress.

Canine Good Citizen

While not a titling event, the AKC Canine Good Citizen program rewards dogs that possess basic training, good manners, and a stable temperament. The training you have done so far and the socializing your dog has experienced should enable him to pass the ten-step test. Once passed, your Cocker is entitled to an AKC certificate and to putting CGC (for Canine Good Citizen) after his name.

These are the tests that your Cocker must pass to earn his CGC:

- Accept a friendly stranger.
- Sit politely for petting.
- Appearance and grooming.
- Walk on a loose lead.

When you have your Cocker's attention, he will keep looking at you despite any distractions.

- Walk through a crowd.
- *Sit* and *down* on command/staying in place.
- *Come* when called.
- Reaction to another dog.
- Reaction to distractions.
- Supervised separation.

The *sit*, *stay*, *down*, and *come* have been discussed in other chapters. Socialization should have accustomed your Cocker to people, other dogs, and distractions. Prior to the test, practice any item you think might be a problem. Many obedience clubs offer the CGC test at the end of a second level class, so you can probably find the CGC at the same place you take your classes.

Rally

Rally is a newer AKC companion event and was intended as an entry point to obedi-

ence and agility competitions (see Chapter 13). It combines the fun and energy of agility with basic obedience exercises without requiring perfect *heel* position. Rally allows more communication with your Cocker than in traditional obedience—you can voice encouragement, repeat commands, pat your leg, and clap your hands. But you cannot touch your dog or use treats.

You and your Cocker progress through a rally course of ten to twenty stations. Each station has a sign that instructs you and your dog to do something involving obedience commands. The signs are numbered to indicate the sequence in which they are done.

We've already discussed several of the obedience commands you and your Cocker will do in rally: *sit*, *down*, *stay*, and *come* (*recall*). Now you can teach and add *finish* to the *recall*.

Finish

Work on lead until your Cocker is reliable with this new exercise. Have your dog *sit*, and tell him to *stay* or *wait*. Many trainers use both *stay* and *wait*, but in different situations. *Stay* means stay right here until I return to you. *Wait* means stay here until I ask you to do something else. They are different from the dog's point of view, and differentiating between them will help him understand and learn.

Tell your dog to *wait*, walk to the end of your lead, and turn around and face your puppy. Call him to you with the *come* command, using lots of encouragement in your voice. You can use the lead to reel him in, and to make sure he comes straight to the front of you. Running backwards a few steps will increase the distance and excitement.

When he arrives in front of you, give him a treat, tell him to *sit*, and another treat would be fine when he does. With the command *finish*, your Cocker will move from sitting in front of you to sitting on your left in *heel* position. Guide him with a treat or toy.

The move to your side can be done in one of two ways. He can walk around on your right, behind and around you, and end up sitting on your left side. An alternate finish is to move from the front directly to your left side; he'll have to turn around in process in order to be sitting at your left and facing the same direction as you. Some dogs actually jump up and turn to get into position.

When he's got the concept, you can add the command *"Finish!"* Remember to give him a treat and lots of praise each time.

Rally Levels

There are three levels of rally competition based on difficulty level. Rally novice is done entirely with your Cocker on lead, has ten to fifteen stations, and only novice signs may be used. Rally advanced is done entirely off lead, has from twelve to seventeen stations, includes one jump, and can use novice or advanced signs; a minimum of three must be advanced stations. The rally excellent class is also done off leash (except

A dog who will reliably *down* and *stay* can go almost everywhere and be welcomed.

for the honor exercise), has fifteen to twenty stations, two jump stations, and can use any signs, but must have at least two excellent level signs and at least three advanced level signs. In rally excellent, handlers are no longer allowed to pat their legs or clap their hands to encourage their dogs.

The rally excellent also includes the honor exercise. In this, your dog must

---

COCKER CLUE

Smart trainers "proof" their Cockers when they train. They add distractions and train in less-than-perfect conditions to acclimate their dogs to perform in most any situation. When he is entered in a trial, where the people, dogs, and place will be different, he is more likely to succeed.

either *sit-stay* or *down-stay* (as specified by the judge) in the rally ring while another dog is running through the course, doing the exercises at each station.

Rally Titles

You can earn rally titles by entering, competing, and receiving a passing score in the three levels of rally classes. A passing score is called a "leg," and three legs at a level earns the title. The titles include Rally Novice or RN, Rally Advanced or RA, and Rally Excellent or RE.

Rally Classes

Basic obedience classes will instruct in the commands that you will need in rally. Rally-specific classes let you practice on the different signs, doing combinations you wouldn't find in a regular obedience trial.

Obedience Competition

Obedience training lets you pursue two goals at once: a well-behaved family pet and impressive titles.

Companion Dog

The training you have done thus far has prepared you for the first level obedience title—that of Companion Dog or CD. The CD title is earned by getting three legs in the novice class exercises in obedience trials. The novice class exercises are heel on

---

COCKER CLUE

Rally stations are represented by signs with words and symbols telling you what to do with your Cocker. Only AKC approved signs can be used. Some signs can be used in all three rally classes, some for advanced and excellent, and some only for excellent. They include

- Halt-Sit
- Halt-Down
- Right Turn
- Left Turn
- About Turn—Right
- About "U" Turn
- 270° Right Turn
- 270° Left Turn
- 360° Right Turn
- 360° Left Turn
- Call Dog Front—Finish Right—Forward
- Call Dog Front—Finish Left—Forward
- Slow Pace
- Fast Pace
- Moving Side Step Right
- Spiral Right, Dog Outside
- Straight Figure 8 Weave Twice

As you can see, a challenge and part of the fun is your understanding what is to be done as well as having your dog do it.

---

lead and off lead, figure eight, stand for exam, recall, long sit, and long down.

The stand for exam exercise requires that you tell your Cocker to *stand* and *stay* while you walk about eight feet beyond him. The judge approaches and touches your dog on the head, shoulders, and back.

The Figure Eight exercise has you walk your Cocker on lead in *heel* position in a figure eight pattern around two people standing about eight feet apart. Heeling with your Cocker will include left, right, and about turns; changing pace, and stopping with your dog sitting in *heel* position. The recall has your dog coming when called from across the ring, sitting in front of you, and then finishing in *heel* position.

Most of the exercises are done with just you, your Cocker, and the judge in the ring. The long sit and long down are done as group exercises, with other dogs in the ring with your Cocker. You dog has to do a long sit (*sit-stay*) for one minute and a long down (*down-stay*) for three minutes, each with you standing across the ring.

Companion Dog Excellent

The next obedience level is Companion Dog Excellent (CDX) and includes exercises that are done in the open class at obedience trials. Three legs will earn your Cocker his CDX title. All exercises are done off lead. The exercises include the heel free and figure eight, drop on recall, retrieve on flat, retrieve over the high jump, broad jump, and long sit and down.

The long sit is extended to three minutes and the long down is five minutes. In the open sit and down exercises, the handlers leave the ring. So when you practice *sit-stay* and *down-stay* with your Cocker, go out of his sight periodically so he will be practiced staying when he cannot see you.

Drop on recall starts like the normal recall. But while your Cocker is en route to you, he is given the *down* command. He must lie down—or *drop*—in mid-recall,

and stay *down* until you call him again to *come* to you.

Practice this in small steps. Stand in front of him while giving the *down* command, verbally and with a hand signal. The advantage to training with both is that your Cocker may respond faster to the arm signal, so that he drops before he gets to you. Bit by bit, practice farther from him until he reliably *downs* at a distance. When he will do that, call him to you. As soon as he is up and starting to you, give him the *down* command. He will initially be confused, but will grow to understand with practice.

Retrieve

CDX exercises include having your dog retrieve. Some Cockers are natural retrievers, but you still want to teach yours to do it when you want him to. Break the retrieve down into parts: running toward a desired object, picking it up, carrying it, returning to you, and giving you the object. Make the sessions very short and

Proud of his dumbbell.

Flying over the bar jump.

exciting, lavish praise and treats, and always leave him wanting more. Construct the lessons so that he always succeeds.

Begin as early as possible with your puppy and make it a game. Start by encouraging him to carry things he likes, such as a stuffed toy, sock, or canvas dummy. You can use the command *take it* when you give him something you want him to carry.

To make him eager to retrieve, hold him back with one hand on his chest, and tease him a few inches from his face with a favored toy. When he eagerly wants it, toss it just a foot or two in front of him and release him to get it. As he learns the concept, practice tossing it farther away.

Use the *recall* to have him bring it back to you. Practice the retrieve down a long hall where he has no choice but to return

toward you with the prize. Initially, use a lead, long line, or flexi-lead to encourage him to return to you. Don't take the ball or dummy from him yet. He got it fairly; it's his. Praise him lots for bringing it to you.

Eventually, he will let you have it. Always reward your Cocker for giving his prize to you. You can offer him something that is at least equally attractive in return for his giving you the retrieved object. If he gets something less or if the game ends, he'll have no incentive to give you his toy or ball.

You want your puppy to hold the object until you've asked him to *give* it to you. You don't want him to drop it in front of you. So don't praise or reward if he drops it, only after you've taken it from his mouth. If he drops it, have him *take it* again, then tell him to *give*, and you take it from him—and give him treats and praise and possibly another toy in return.

Don't practice more than three or four retrieves in one session. Always leave him wanting more.

Jumps

CDX exercises include both a high jump and a broad jump. To practice jumps, use the equipment found in most obedience clubs or schools, or get your own.

In obedience trials, there are prescribed heights and breadths for jumps. The high jump will be set at your dog's shoulder height rounded to the nearest 2-inch increment. The broad jump will cover a distance twice the height of the high jump.

In practice, use much shorter jumps to teach the concept—just four to eight inches tall for the high jump and a hurdle or two placed close together. Initially, go over the jump with him. Make it exciting; lure him with treats. Having him on lead, progress to encouraging him to jump over and back. Gradually increase the height. Height isn't the main issue; he can adjust to a taller height later. Important is his biddability.

Using a low jump, you can encourage him to retrieve over the jump. He will be more likely to return back over the jump, if you put up some kind of fence so that he cannot go around it.

Utility

Utility is the highest level of AKC obedience. If you and your Cocker enjoy training, it is an attainable goal. It takes three legs to earn the Utility Dog (UD) title. Your dog will need to do several exercises—*heel*, *sit*, *down*, and *come*—with hand signals only. The directed retrieve has your dog retrieve the one glove of three that you point to. Directed jumping has him jump over the one jump (of two) that you indicate. The most impressive is scent discrimination, in which your Cocker retrieves the one dumbbell among eight that has your scent on it.

One of the challenges of utility is that many of the exercises require your Cocker to leave you (*go out*). Most obedience exercises are done with your dog close and (possibly) easier to control. Now, we're sending our dog away to perform on his own.

If you and your Cocker enjoy obedience and want to work toward obedience titles, find and join an obedience club. Most of

Many trainers begin to teach exercises for open and utility while their Cocker is still in novice, to keep them and their dogs from getting bored.

the members are actively training and competing with their dogs. They are a great source of information, and can offer advice on what works, and alternate methods for your dog. They offer classes, usually at a discount to members. The classes are taught by club members—maybe you will be one of the instructors one day. Those working on advanced titles often meet to train together and are very supportive of each others' successes, commiserating when things don't go quite right. Great people with great dogs—what could be better?

Home Schooling

Tracking

Your Cocker Spaniel already knows how to follow a scent. He comes with the required equipment—a canine nose with a sense of smell that is 100,000 times stronger than yours. All you have to do is communicate to your Cocker which smell you want him to focus on and that you want him to follow it.

When you walk, you shed bits of skin, perspiration, and fabric fibers. They float toward the ground, with some lingering in the air. As you walk, you disturb the ground. Grass, leaves, twigs, and dirt are crushed, moved, and stirred around. Your Cocker can follow the trail of these smells. If there is a bit of moisture, like the morning dew, the odors are enhanced. Think of the difference in smell between raw, dry cabbage and cabbage in boiling water. As your Cocker's ears brush on or near the ground, they stir up the scent and make it more available to his nose.

AKC Tracking Tests

AKC's tracking tests provide recognition to dogs who demonstrate their natural ability to find and follow a scent. The tests are non-competitive. Unlike many other events, your Cocker only needs to complete one track to earn each title.

There are three tracking titles offered by AKC. The Tracking Dog (TD) title is the initial one. For the TD, your Cocker must follow a track about 440–500 yards long with three to five turns. The track will have been made from thirty minutes to two hours before the track is run.

The second level is the Tracking Dog Excellent (TDX). The TDX title requires your dog to follow a track that is three to five hours old and 800 to 1,000 yards long, with five to seven changes in direction.

The TD and TDX tracks are laid through grass or similar vegetation. The third level is Variable Surface Tracking (VST). This requires your Cocker to follow a track in an urban setting, over pavement, asphalt, bricks, and areas with no vegetation. Any dog that has successfully earned all three tracking titles can claim the title of Champion Tracker or CT.

Equipment

Minimum equipment is needed for tracking. Your Cocker will wear a nylon harness so that when he pulls along the track, the pressure will be on his chest, not around his neck. A long line, ten to forty feet long, clipped to a ring on the harness along his back will allow him to range in front of you. Dowels or similar items can be used to mark the trail for us poor humans who can't smell well enough to locate it. You will also need a glove to place at the end of the trail for your Cocker to find.

There are different opinions about using food. If your Cocker is highly food motivated, try it. You can smear some on the bottom of your shoes as you lay the track to enhance the scent. You can lay tidbits of treats along the track to incent your dog to follow it. As he gets the concept, you can space the treats farther apart.

How to Train

If you can find others to work with, you can share the effort and the fun. Find a field you can work in that is fairly flat and mowed. Try to work early in the morning when the ground may be damp and when the place doesn't have other people already walking on it, laying their own tracks and distracting your dog.

Confine your dog while you lay the track. Lay your initial track by shuffling your feet in place at the beginning. Proceed forward in a straight line shuffling your feet. After about twenty feet from the start, place the glove with a treat on top of it for your dog to find. Shuffle back along the same path, to both strengthen that path and to not lay another. If you have smeared anything on the bottom of your shoes to lay the track, change shoes before walking elsewhere.

Get your dog, in harness and on lead. Point to and touch the beginning of the track. Get him to smell it. Encourage him along the track if he hasn't found it. If he is following it, keep quiet, don't distract him, and let him concentrate. If he gets off the track, bring him back to the point he left, and show it to him again.

You can do perhaps three tracks in a practice, depending on how long they are. Always stop before he is tired or bored. Whenever possible, stop when he has been successful.

As your Cocker gets the concept, make the tracks longer. Introduce a turn, initially no more than a forty-five degree angle. You can later add a second turn or a more abrupt turn. When he understands tracking, trust your dog. This is one event where he is in charge and better able to follow the track than you.

Natural Tracker

Tracking uses a Cocker's natural talent. Some are better than others, as with everything else. You can start tracking training with a puppy as early as three months. If you are already introducing your Cocker to birds for hunting or if he is naturally birdy, realize that there may be birds on the property you are using for tracking that will distract him. It will be hard for him to ignore birds to stay on a track until he understands better what tracking is all about. On the other hand, practicing using his nose to follow a scent can support his bird-finding skills in hunting.

Encourage your puppy to use his nose by playing a game where you hide a treat and ask him to find it. Make it easy at first while he is still learning.

12 *Showing Your Cocker Spaniel*

If you plan to show your Cocker Spaniel, tell your breeder before you get your puppy so he can help you select a show-quality puppy. Conformation dog shows identify those dogs that conform the most to the breed standard, a written description of the perfect dog for that breed. The judge looks at the dog's head and expression, coat color and texture, the shape, proportions, and structure, her movement, and temperament. The winner will be the dog that the judge thinks is closest to a perfect Cocker Spaniel showing that day.

You want to get a show-potential puppy from a breeder who shows dogs, who had bred many champions, and from a litter where most of the parents, grandparents, and even great-grandparents are champions. Let your breeder pick out the puppy for you, for he will be better able to evaluate her potential as a show dog.

Dog Shows

The original purpose of dog shows was to evaluate breeding stock and identify the better prospects to be used to produce the next generation. Many folks, even if they don't intend to breed, enjoy the competition with their dogs. It is a family sport and involves dog lovers of all ages.

Championships

The title you can earn by showing your Cocker is her championship. Most breeds compete against others in the same breed and of the same sex to earn points towards this end. Cocker Spaniels are divided into three color groups called varieties: black (which includes black with tan points), ASCOB (any solid color other than black), and parti-color (white and one other solid color). Cockers compete against those in the same variety, rather than breed, and the same gender for points.

Your puppy must be at least six months old to enter and compete at a dog show. She needs to earn fifteen points to earn her championship, including two majors. A major is a win worth three, four, or five points. How many points are won at a show depends on the number competing that day of the same variety and sex as your puppy; the more Cockers competing, the more points can be won, up to a maximum of five points at one show.

COCKER CLUE

The judge evaluates your and the other Cockers competing against the breed standard. The important criteria from the Cocker Spaniel standard are

- *Height of 15" for an adult male or 14" for an adult female, measured at the top of the shoulder. Males over 15½" and females over 14" are disqualified.*
- *Round, full, and dark brown eyes.*
- *Long, well feathered ears, placed no higher than eye level.*
- *Rounded skull.*
- *Broad, deep muzzle with square even jaws.*
- *Teeth meeting in a scissors bite. The top incisors barely overlap, but touch the lower incisors.*
- *Slightly sloping topline.*
- *Parallel, straight, and strongly boned forelegs.*
- *Compact, large feet, turning neither in or out.*
- *Well-angulated forequarters, moderately angulated hindquarters.*
- *Silky, flat, or slightly wavy coat.*
- *Equable, merry temperament: Tail wags when dog is in motion.*
- *Black, parti-colored, or ASCOB.*

Grooming at an outside dog show before going to the ring.

Conformation Training

Conformation classes teach you and your Cocker how to compete at a dog show. There are several things to learn, including stacking, gaiting, and baiting your Cocker.

You will use a show lead when training and presenting your Cocker. A slip lead or martingale, in which the collar and lead are combined into one unit, are most common. The lead portion is three to four feet long. The collar is normally kept high on the dog's neck, kept in place by the slip part of the lead or the second loop of the martingale. This keeps the dog's head held high and shows off her neck.

Stacking, or setting up, your Cocker means posing her in a fairly natural stance so that she will look beautiful for the judge. You bring the collar high on her neck so that you can control her head while adjusting her feet. Place her front feet so that they are directly under the

A Cocker's ears wrapped in vet wrap to keep the coat from being mussed. The wraps are removed before entering the show ring.

The judge or conformation class instructor will examine Cockers individually on a grooming table in the show ring. Lift your dog to place and stack her on the table. Practice placing your puppy so that as many of her legs as possible come down where you want them stacked, remembering to keep the collar high and her head up. Your goal is to have her look like she is seeing a bird, just before she runs to get it.

When the judge looks at all the Cockers in a class, the handlers will have their dogs stacked in a line on the ground. You will need to kneel down behind your dog and stack her on the ground as you did on the table.

Dress appropriately to show your dog. Wear sensible shoes that you can easily walk fast or trot in. Men wear suits or trousers with sports coats. Women wear sporty suits or pants outfits. The color of your clothes should enhance your Cocker. If your Cocker is black, don't wear dark colored clothes, because the judge won't be able to see your dog. If you have a parti-colored Cocker, don't wear a print that will clash with your dog and make the judge dizzy looking at the two of you.

Practice setting your Cocker up both on the table and on the ground. Stack her in front of a mirror so you can see what the judge will see.

The judge will ask you to gait your dog. This involves having your puppy trot at your left side in one of several patterns in the ring. You will have to move at a speed that will result in your dog trotting, not walking or galloping, to keep up with you. The judge will see how well your dog moves and whether she still looks as nice

top of her shoulder blades, pointing straight ahead, with her front legs parallel to each other. Place her front feet by holding her elbow rather than some other part of her leg. Place her rear feet slightly wider apart than her front feet and extended back so that the hock (the bone above the rear foot) is perpendicular to the floor. Place her rear feet by either holding the hock itself or the stifle (knee) of each rear leg.

The judge examines a dog stacked on the table. Notice the ears are pulled forward to show off the neck and neck set.

as when you set her up. Practice gaiting with your Cocker so that you move smoothly together, at a speed where she looks her best.

Baiting involves showing your dog a tiny piece of food so that she looks alert, up on her toes. Your dog is always standing in the dog show ring; no sitting is allowed. If you are going to show your Cocker, never teach her to *sit* for a treat. When she sees the bait or treat, she should stand tall and stretch a bit, in hopes of getting a tiny bit of the bait.

Practice baiting at home so that she will self-stack in anticipation of getting a treat. Give her a tiny piece of the treat once in awhile to reinforce good dog show performance. You aren't feeding her, though, just teasing and enticing her with the bait.

Matches

Matches are practice dog shows that get both dog and handler accustomed to the show ring. The judges are also in training as they aren't currently approved by AKC to judge. Contact dog clubs in your area to learn when and where matches are held, and enter your Cocker to practice.

Conditioning

In order for your dog to win, she needs to be built correctly, presented competently, and be in good condition. Condition refers to good health, toned muscles, proper weight for her size, and well-cared-for coat.

You are in charge of your Cocker's diet and exercise. High-quality food will contribute to her good overall health, musculature, and glossy coat. Check her weight regularly, and add or decrease her food as necessary. Cockers are food hounds, so she may be too chubby. Keep her at good weight not only for appearance, but for good health. Obesity causes as many problems in dogs as it does in people.

Regular exercise is good for both body and soul. Daily exercise will expend your Cocker's extra energy and help her to be more focused during training as well as more relaxed in the house. A well-muscled dog will move better, and stand better in the show ring. The judge will check your dog's musculature during the examination.

A Cocker's coat is her crowning glory and will contribute heavily to her chances of winning. It should be properly trimmed for the show ring, clean and freshly brushed, and cared for with coat products that will make it look its best.

Trimming and bathing will be done at home before the show, but you will be brushing her at the show before going in the ring. Bring your equipment to the show: grooming table (a small one more easily managed), combs and brushes, and a misting bottle filled with water and a bit of conditioner. There are grooming areas at each show where you can set up

your equipment and do last-minute preparation for the ring. Many handlers take a pin brush into the ring for touch-ups if the coat gets mussed.

Show Attitude

Socialization is part of conditioning, and developing your Cocker's show attitude can make a big difference in your success in the ring. A Cocker is a merry little spaniel, and the judge will consider your dog's temperament and character to see if it is correct for a Cocker. A happy dog with a wagging tail shows that she is confident, proud, and enjoys being a show dog.

Develop this attitude by introducing your Cocker early on to many different

> **COCKER CLUE**
>
> Junior showmanship is a competition at dog shows where youngsters demonstrate their abilities to present their dogs. Classes are divided by age and experience of the youngster.
>
> - Novice Junior 9–12 years.
> - Novice Intermediate 12–15 years.
> - Novice Senior 15–18 years.
> - Open Junior 9–12 years.
> - Open Intermediate 12–15 years.
> - Open Senior 15–18 years.
>
> Junior showmanship introduces and encourages Juniors in the sport of dogs. It provides a competition where youngsters can learn and improve their handling skills. Displaying good sportsmanship is also stressed.

people and places. Have her meet people of all shapes and sizes, races and nationalities, wearing different clothing, including extra jewelry, big or strange hats, big, long, and flowing coats. With these experiences under her collar, your Cocker should encounter all the commotion of a dog show with equanimity.

Have as many different people as possible go over your puppy as a dog show judge would. Have them look at her teeth, handle her ears, touch her all over. If your Cocker is male, have them check his testicles. When your dog gets to the show ring and the judge goes over her, she will be accustomed to handling and welcome the attention.

Handling Your Cocker

Cockers love being the center of attention.

You can show your Cocker yourself or you can hire a professional handler.

If you want to do the showing yourself, watch experienced and professional handlers to see what they do to make their dogs look good. Practice these techniques at home and in handling classes.

Some owners aren't comfortable taking their dogs into the show ring. They may be nervous or not athletic enough to show their own dog and prefer to sit ringside and watch someone else make their dog look good. If you feel this way, you can hire a professional handler. The handler will take your dog into the ring and may also groom her at the show as well. There is much to learn from skilled professional handlers who specialize in Cocker Spaniels.

Talk to other Cocker owners who show their dogs and ask for recommendations. Watch Cockers being shown, making notes of which handlers do the best job and treat the dogs well and gently.

You can talk to a handler at a show when he has a break, or you can contact him between shows. Get a rate sheet to understand what the costs are. Ask the handler what his terms are. How does he manage the situation when he is handling more than one Cocker? What does he do when he has a conflict and is scheduled to show another dog in another ring? Determine whether you or the handler sends in the show entries. Will the handler groom

your Cocker as well, and if so, what is the charge for that? Get as much determined ahead of time to avoid misunderstandings.

Dog Clubs

If you enjoy dog shows, you may want to join a local dog club. Most are looking for new members to help with the many tasks involved in putting on a dog show, such as arranging for trophies, selling catalogs, helping with hospitality, and much more. Dog clubs are also a great way to get to know others interested in dogs and dog shows. Many present programs at meetings to inform and educate members and guests.

There are multiple kinds of dog clubs for you to investigate. All-breed dog clubs put on dog shows; their members will each have one or more of the AKC-recognized breeds.

Specialty clubs are for people involved in a single breed, such as Cocker Spaniels. Specialty clubs put on shows for one breed only. There are many specialty clubs, especially in the more popular breeds like Cocker Spaniels.

Each breed also has a national breed or parent club. For Cockers, this is the American Spaniel Club (*www. asc-cockerspaniel.org*). The club puts on two national specialty shows a year, one open to all flushing spaniels and one limited to Cocker Spaniels. All of the local Cocker Spaniel specialty clubs are affiliated with the national club.

Some dog clubs put on only conformation dog shows. Others include obedience, rally, and obedience trials at their events, depending upon the interests and ambitions of their members.

Most dog club meetings are open to guests. Attend and consider joining. You'll see a whole different side to dog shows.

13 *Agility*

Agility is one of the most popular and rapidly growing AKC events. Fun for both dogs and handlers, it's also fast and exciting for spectators. Agility is easy for the uninitiated to follow.

The sport is based on stadium jumping competitions for horses. A dog teamed with a handler runs a complex course of obstacles. They are judged on both speed and accuracy. Faults, such as doing an obstacle incorrectly, knocking down a jump, following the wrong sequence, refusing an obstacle, or not touching required contact surfaces, are penalized.

Some obstacles are sized for the size division of the dogs, such as jump heights and lengths. Cockers may be entered in the 12-inch or 16-inch class in AKC agility. A-frame, teeter (seesaw), tunnels, pause table, weave poles, and other obstacles are the same for all breeds. You can simulate some of these in your yard for practice.

Many obedience/agility training clubs have agility obstacles set up and offer classes. Classes are tailored to different levels, including puppy and beginner as well as more advanced teams. Most use positive reinforcement, rewarding the dogs with treats, toys, or balls—whatever is the best lure and motivator for the individual dogs.

Getting Started

Cocker Spaniels that are confident, focused on their owners, and have a healthy prey drive are good candidates for agility. Dogs should be healthy and structurally sound, to better handle the speed and jumping involved.

Expose your Cocker to agility obstacles early. Let him explore and investigate them and become comfortable around them. Dogs learn much by watching other dogs so take him to trials to watch. Let him get acquainted with the sights, smells, and sounds, the other dogs, and the overall excitement and noise. One sound that startles some dogs is the banging of the teeter. If he is shy, let him become accustomed at a comfortable distance, slowly getting closer as he adjusts to the sounds and excitement.

Playgrounds are a great place to familiarize your Cocker with odd-looking equipment. Let him climb on the structures if he can do so safely. Show him the seesaw, ladders, and steps.

A strong obedience training foundation is prerequisite for agility training. You must have your Cocker's attention. He needs to work with you, even though he is working physically away from you.

For instance, you may tell him "Go weave" as you progress to the end of the obstacle. A reliable *recall* as well as *sit, down,* and *stay* are required.

Maturity

Agility is a physical sport for your Cocker. Not only must he be in condition, he must also be physically mature—at least one year of age—before starting strenuous training. Make sure growth plates (the ends of the bones where new bone is created) are closed, as this is the weakest part of the bone before growth is completed. Serious injury can result from falling off an A-frame or dog-walk. Landing after a jump is traumatic on your dog's front assembly and shouldn't be done until his skeleton has finished growing. Weave poles can stress a dog's body before the ligaments and muscles along the spine are ready. Make sure your Cocker athlete is ready and in condition for the exertions in agility.

While you are waiting for him to be mature, work on basic obedience. Teach direction training, so you can instruct him to turn or go to a particular obstacle. Make sure his *recall* is reliable even with distractions.

Opinions differ as to when it is safe to start specific activities. You can introduce modified versions of some obstacles that are safer for your dog. You can use very low jumps—just a few inches—and have your dog land on soft ground. A dog walk set just a few inches off the ground will accustom him to the obstacle with no danger of falling.

Contact Zones

Teach your Cocker about contacts—spots where the dog must touch the yellow

The following are classes that you can enter at an AKC agility trial. Three qualifying scores earn the title in the first three classes: ten qualifying scores are required for the Master title.

- Novice Agility (NA)
- Open Agility (OA)
- Agility Excellent A (AX)
- Master Agility Excellent (MX)

portion of the A-frame, dog-walk, and teeter before leaving the obstacle. Teach him to stop in the contact portion, to touch the contact portion, and stay there until you say "Okay." Put treats in the contact zone, using the plastic lid from a food container to hold them. He gets the reward only when he touches the contact zone.

Training Obstacles

Consider getting your own equipment to train your dog in agility. Some may be inexpensive; others you can construct yourself. Use obstacles that you can lower closer to the ground or are smaller versions of standard obstacles to begin training.

As you train on each obstacle and your Cocker becomes familiar with it, name the obstacle—table, walk it, hoop or tire, weave—so you can name the next obstacle in sequence that you want him to do in the course. Use the obstacle name every time from the first time your Cocker is introduced to it. Remember that your dog will be much faster than you and

needs to get to the next obstacle without your physically guiding him to it.

The obstacles are listed below. Next to each is a word you might use to name the obstacle for your Cocker.

Pause Table (Table)

The pause table is as tall as the height division allows (12 or 16 inches for Cocker Spaniels) and three feet square, with a non-skid surface. Your Cocker must jump up onto the table and *sit* or *down* for five seconds before proceeding to the next obstacle.

You need to teach your dog to jump up onto the table. Pat the table, encouraging your Cocker to jump up on it. You can put a small treat on the table that he can only reach from the tabletop. If height concerns him, start with a lower table.

Make sure it is secure and sturdy. Being on a wobbly table is enough to discourage a dog from trying again. You've already taught the *sit*, *down*, and *stay*. So what you need to do is to practice your Cocker's doing them on the pause table.

You may have to say the commands *table-sit* (or *table-down*) so that your dog, in his enthusiasm, doesn't jump down as soon as he jumps up. Count slowly from 1 to 5 for the five seconds, and release and treat your dog.

Jumps (Jump)

There are two types of high jumps, the panel jump and the bar jump. The panel jump presents a solid wall for your Cocker to jump over. The bar jump consists of bars held in place by upright supports. It may have one bar or two or more. The bar jump is considered harder since your

Posing on the pause table.

dog can see through it, making it seem less of an obstacle to be jumped. The height of the jumps vary with the height division your Cocker is running in. Your Cocker must jump over the jump without knocking any part down. These are effectively the same jumps done in obedience.

Tire Jump (Tire)

The tire jump has a tire or some circular item that looks like a tire hung in a rectangular frame. The circular opening must be about two feet in diameter. Your Cocker must jump through the opening without knocking it down.

The challenge is to accustom your Cocker to a visually different jump. He won't automatically assume that the behavior is the same wanted with the other jumps.

Initially hold the tire (or something that resembles one) vertically but touching the ground. Lure your Cocker through the opening, using the word "Tire." This is one jump you can't go over with your dog. Raise the tire gradually as he gets accustomed to going through it. You teach him two concepts, one at a time: through the tire, then adding the height to jump through it.

Broad Jump (Broad)

This broad jump is much the same as the one used in obedience. The length of the jump is twice the jump height of the height division that your Cocker is running in.

Start by having your dog jump across just one jump board. You go with him and use a treat to lure him. When he is comfortable doing that, add another board, gradually building up to the distance he will have to jump. When you can no longer jump with him, you can put the treat on the lid of a margarine tub on the far side of the boards, to reward him for doing the jump.

A-Frame (A-frame)

The A-frame looks like the letter "A." It is made of two panels hinged at the top, each panel about nine feet long. The bottom of the panels are spread so that the height of the A-frame is about five and a half feet. The surface of the panels on which the dogs walk is non-slip and has slats placed across the width about a foot apart to give the dogs footing. It has a contact zone on the bottom 42 inches of each panel. Your Cocker needs to go up one panel, over the tallest part, and descend the down side of the A-frame. At least one foot must touch the contact zone before leaving the obstacle.

How fast you can train on the A-frame will depend on how comfortable your Cocker is with the obstacle and walking up and down inclines. You could make a much shorter version to practice on. Or you could spread the panel bottoms farther apart to make the incline much less steep. Make sure they are stable, though, and won't collapse when your Cocker walks on it.

With your Cocker on lead, guide him to, up, and over the A-frame or miniature

version making sure he touches the contact zone before getting off. Lure him with food or a toy. He gets his reward when he touches the contact.

Open Tunnel (Tunnel)

The tunnel is a flexible tube than can be formed into curved shapes. The tunnel and the openings are about two feet in diameter, with the overall length being 10 to 20 feet long.

Your Cocker will enter through the designated end and exit through the other. It isn't as challenging for a Cocker as it is for larger breeds, for Cockers can easily run through without ducking or crouching.

To practice with the tunnel, compress it to its shortest length. Have someone hold your Cocker at one end, while you look through the other and entice him with a treat or toy. Gradually lengthen the tunnel for him to run through. When he is comfortable going through the longer tunnel, add a slight bend so he can't see the entire exit opening. Bend it further so that eventually he cannot see the exit from the entrance. By now he knows there is a treat at the end, and should run through just fine.

Closed Tunnel (Chute)

The closed tunnel begins like the open tunnel with a rigid opening, but then changes into a chute made of material or fabric. The overall length of the closed tunnel is about 12 feet. Your Cocker must enter the rigid opening and push his way through the fabric chute to exit the other end.

Teach it slowly, starting with the fabric completely gathered up towards the rigid end so your Cocker can see through the

Practicing the weave poles.

tunnel. Gradually let more fabric hang down as he learns that the material can be shoved out of the way as he goes through. Eventually, he won't be able to see through the hanging fabric, but will know how to push through. Very slowly lengthen the chute so he is not just pushing through a flap but through a short fabric tunnel. Gradually lengthen the chute until he can push his way through the full length.

Dog Walk (Walk-it)

The dog walk is a 12-inch wide plank with a ramp leading up one end and another leading down at the other. In competition the center section is four feet off the ground. It is better to have the plank much lower to the ground while your Cocker is in training. There are contact zones at the beginning of the up ramp and the end of the down ramp.

Practice lead luring your dog up the ramp, across the plank, and down the exit ramp. He gets the treat only when touching the ending contact. If he gets down, start over. Don't get back on in the middle of the plank.

Teeter-totter or Seesaw (Teeter)

The agility seesaw is just those on playgrounds. The plank is about a foot wide, with a fulcrum about two feet off the ground. There are contact zones at each end, both of which your Cocker must touch. If possible, make a shorter version for practice, with the fulcrum much closer to the ground. You can adjust it progressively higher as he gets the concept.

Your Cocker must go up the plank touching the ground, go to the center causing the plank to pivot, and then go down the other side. During training, when your dog passes the fulcrum, hold the rising end of the plank so that the part the dog is going down doesn't move too quickly and bump or bounce on the ground. A bounce may startle the dog and make him lose his footing, turning him off from the obstacle.

From your Cocker's point of view, the dog walk and the teeter look the same: they both start with up ramps. Make sure that your dog hears the name of the obstacle so he knows what is coming at the top of the ramp.

The teeter is a more foreign obstacle to dogs and it will take longer for your Cocker to become accustomed to it. Take it slowly, with practice, patience, and lots of treats.

Weave Poles (Weave)

Weave poles are multiple upright fixed poles about 40 inches high, spaced in a straight line about 20 to 24 inches apart.

Your Cocker enters the weave poles by passing between pole number one and two from right to left. Then he goes between pole two and three from left to right. He continues the weaving pattern until he goes between the last two poles.

Line the weave poles in a staggered position so he can pass through them with little weaving. Start with fewer poles while training. Lure him several times through the path to help him get the concept. Move the poles closer together so that he needs to move his body slightly as you lure him through the path. Reward

your Cocker with each pass. Continue to move the poles closer, practicing at each change. Eventually they will be in a straight line, and the dog will be weaving. You can erect barriers so that he cannot easily leave the sequence, making the weaving pattern the easiest path to take.

As you run the course, you may find the weave poles and your Cocker on your left. This is fine, for when your dog goes between the first two poles, he will be going from right to left. But, he must enter the weave poles from right to left wherever they are, so if the poles are on your right, your dog needs to go to the other side to enter correctly. You may want to use two different commands to let him know which he is doing, *weave* for the poles on your and your Cocker's left, and *right weave* for those on his right.

Weave poles are often the hardest obstacle to teach since there are so many opportunities for your Cocker to leave or do it incorrectly. When he has the idea, add distractions to proof his performance.

Teamwork

Agility isn't simply the art of working obstacles, it also requires the course to be completed in a specific sequence. The course will vary every time. Your Cocker's part of the game is to do the obstacles. Your part is to provide direction—communicating to your partner what and where the next obstacle is.

Provide the direction with your voice—naming the next obstacle—and your body language. Point with your arm and hand and lean your shoulder in the direction of

You cannot touch your dog during a trial or bring food, balls, toys, or the like onto the course. The stress is greater for both you and your Cocker at a trial. Try whatever tricks you can to calm yourself, for your nervousness will transmit to your dog and affect his performance. Stress changes your body chemistry, and your dog can smell it on your breath. A mint or hard candy will help camouflage your anxiety. At the end of the course, whether he qualifies or not, praise your Cocker and tell him how well he did. Cockers are very sensitive to how you feel. He needs you to be happy. So feel good and tell your dog what a good boy he is.

the next obstacle. You must run the course and indicate to your dog what is next. Make sure he finishes the current obstacle before telling him what's next.

When you train and practice, do the obstacles in different sequences. Rearrange the obstacles so your Cocker won't expect the same configuration. Set traps. Put an obstacle that is not next near the end of another. If your direction is good and he is paying attention, your Cocker should proceed to the correct obstacle.

Practice

Train at home and in agility class. Add as many distractions as you can to simulate a real trial. Include other dogs and people, especially children. Honk horns and squeak toys. Play music. Practice inside and out. Take him to agility trials even before you enter so he can acclimate to the environment.

In agility your Cocker works away from you, which makes practice and preparation even more important.

Home Schooling

Flyball

Flyball is exciting for both people and dogs and is one of the fastest-growing dog sports in the United States. Flyball is a relay race between teams of dogs. Each dog runs down a line over several hurdles, gets a ball from a spring-loaded ball box, and runs back down the line to his team while carrying the ball.

Flyball is not an AKC event. Events are held under the auspices of the North American Flyball Association (NAFA), *www.flyball.org*, and the United Flyball League International (UFLI), *www.ufli.com*. Flyball clubs and events are listed on both organizations' Web sites.

What Is Flyball?

Flyball races, also called heats, are competitions between two teams of four dogs each, racing side by side along a 51-foot course. The dogs run a relay, one dog from a team at a time, down the course over a series of jumps. At the end of the course, each dog triggers a flyball box that releases a tennis ball. The dog grabs the ball and returns back over the course and the jumps. When he returns, the next dog is released to do the same. The first team to have all four dogs run and return without errors wins the heat.

The jumps on the course are based on the smallest dog on the team, known as the "height dog." He is measured at the withers. Four inches are deducted from the dog's height; rounded down to the nearest inch, this measurement becomes the height of jumps. Each team needs a fast dog small enough to provide low jump heights. A Cocker is a welcome addition to a team of bigger dogs, since he lowers the jump heights.

All dogs, including mixed breeds, are eligible to compete. Titles are earned based on the speed of the team. For speeds under 24 seconds, each dog on the team gets 25 points; under 28 seconds, 5 points; under 32 seconds, 1 point.

Flyball Titles

Points	Title
■ 20	Flyball Dog (FD)
■ 100	Flyball Dog Excellent (FDX)
■ 500	Flyball Dog Champion (FDCh)

And there are many more . . . .

What Equipment Is Used?

Flyball equipment includes a box that launches the ball when the dog jumps on it. The boxes have more than one hole so that the ball can pop out in the direction in which the dog naturally turns. There are left-handed and right-handed dogs. Tennis balls are most common, but other bouncing balls may be used. Flat collars, slip collars, and harnesses are the only collar types allowed. Each dog on a team may use different types of balls

Cockers with a natural interest in balls are good candidates for flyball.

popping out of different holes from the flyball box.

How Does Flyball Training Begin?

Training for flyball involves breaking down the behaviors into tiny components. Many obedience clubs also teach flyball classes. To begin, your dog needs a solid *recall*. The flyball recall puts the emphasis on speed. You can practice by having someone hold your Cocker; call him to you and run, still calling him. The idea is to encourage him to chase you.

It is helpful if your Cocker is ball motivated. Not too obsessed, though, for your dog might take off after balls of another team. If your dog does not crave balls, you can create the drive. Use clicker training with treats to reward progressive interest in balls, initially just moving toward the ball and touching it to picking it up and carrying it.

Retrieving is another foundation skill for flyball. No forced retrieve is ever used, however. Flyball depends on your Cocker's enthusiasm and excitement, not reluctant compliance. You can practice by having your Cocker retrieve balls. The focus is on speed, so you want him to run full out on his return. As he returns, turn and run, encouraging him to chase and catch up with you.

A small, fast dog is desirable on each flyball team.

How Is the Flyball Box Introduced?

Before introducing your Cocker to the flyball box, teach him to turn. You are aiming for a competitive swimmer's turn for speed. Discover first if your dog naturally turns right or left during a retrieve, then lure him around a cone in his preferred direction. Use with treats as necessary, to show him the turn. Eventually place the flyball box in his path so he will have to touch the box when going around the cone.

Your goal is to get your dog to approach the box and retrieve the ball as part of his turn. The frontal approach is

slower. Initially, the ball is just placed on the box (use Velcro to keep it in place). The dog can run out and retrieve the ball from the top of the box. Later, the ball will be delivered to the dog from the hole. Good dogs will catch the ball in mid-turn just as it comes out of the hole. Catching the ball from a lobbed arc is too slow and subject to errors.

How Early Can Flyball Training Begin?

Training for flyball can start at the puppy stage, but your Cocker cannot compete until he is a year old. You can take your puppy to a flyball event, though, and sit on the sidelines. Let him watch the other dogs run, hear the noise, feel the excitement. He'll catch the spirit early.

Teamwork

Flyball really is a team effort. It isn't just you and your Cocker. A team consists of six people and six dogs and a box loader. Some teams keep two of the dogs as back-up runners; others rotate the dogs in the multiple heats that run during the event. The box loader must know the order the dogs will be run in each heat, the type of ball each dog retrieves, and the hole each dog expects the ball to launch from. Remember that a race is run by four dogs in a half-minute or less, so there is no time to think. The box loader must be prepared.

If you and your Cocker have the energy and love the excitement of competition, try flyball. It's great fun, and great exercise, too.

14 Hunt and Field

Cocker Spaniels, the smallest sporting breed, were developed to find and flush birds. Today, they retain the instinct to hunt. Paired with their merry temperament and willingness to please, they make excellent hunting partners.

Cockers hunt at a moderate pace. When they find game, their active body movements and rapidly wagging tail indicate the find. Cockers are particularly good at hunting upland game birds in dense cover. They mark well for their size and can retrieve bigger birds than one would expect.

While more Cocker Spaniels are registered with AKC than any other spaniel, Cockers are one of the least represented in spaniel hunt and field events. Many mistakenly believe that the longer coat on show Cockers makes them unsuitable for the field. Other hunters want a bigger, stronger spaniel. Field performance events are competitive, and those focused on the competition pick the most competitive breeds. But coats can be trimmed, the Cocker's small size was designed for getting into dense cover, and the breed retains its desire and willingness to hunt. So, if you are inclined, pursue the one activity your Cocker was bred to do.

Hunt Tests

AKC hunt tests encourage hunters to develop good hunting dogs by evaluating the dog's ability to perform at three different levels. They are open to nine spaniel breeds: American Water Spaniel, Boykin Spaniels, Clumber Spaniels, Cocker Spaniels, English Cocker Spaniels, English Springer Spaniels, Field Spaniels, Sussex Spaniels, and Welsh Springer Spaniels.

Hunt tests are not competitive; your Cocker doesn't have to best other dogs. There are separate hunt tests for the different classifications of sporting breeds, such as spaniels, retrievers, and pointers. The dogs are measured against a standard, and when the requirements for the level are met, the dog is awarded the title JH for Junior Hunter, SH or Senior Hunter, and MH for Master Hunter.

Unlike some other events, you can enter your Cocker in any level you want to compete in without achieving qualifying scores or titles at the lower levels. Four qualifying scores or legs are required for the JH title. Five legs are required for SH, or only four if your dog has her JH title. Five legs for the Master Hunter, or six legs if she doesn't have the SH title.

Small breed, big retrieve.

of the event. Go to an actual hunt test and watch the dogs to see how they work. If you want to follow the dogs, wear suitable footwear for the rough territory. To be on the field, at least one article of your clothing, usually a vest or jacket, must be blaze orange in color. You can find the locations of the clubs, seminars, and hunt tests on the AKCs Web site, *www.akc.org.*

Field Trials

Some owners are committed to maintaining and confirming their Cocker's hunting instinct and earn at least the Junior Hunter title. Some progress to higher titles. But fewer Cocker Spaniels compete in spaniel field trials. English Springer Spaniels are prominent in those events, with the Cockers represented by English Cocker Spaniels.

A field trial is a performance event put on by AKC members or licensed clubs. Points are awarded towards a field championship. Dogs are entered and compete in one of the regular stakes offered: Puppy, Novice, Limit, Open All-Age or Qualified Open All-Age, and Amateur All-Age. There is also a National Champion Stake for Cocker Spaniels, including English Cockers, run once per year.

Dogs must be under control at all times. They are judged on their scenting ability, how they cover ground, the intensity with which they approach cover, their steadiness, how well they retrieve and deliver birds, their soft mouth, ability to mark and find the birds, and the ability to work from hand signals.

In AKC hunt tests, dogs are evaluated on their hunting ability, ability to find birds, retrieving ability, and how well they are trained or how well they respond to their handler's commands.

To learn about hunting, find and visit a local hunt club in your area. Attend an AKC hunting test seminar to learn what your dog will be judged on, the requirements for titles, and rules and regulations

Hunting Cocker Spaniels

A good Cocker candidate for hunting should have an intense desire to work, good structure to last in the field, and a strong instinct to hunt. She cannot be afraid or shy, and should be biddable with a bit of independence. Some characteristics sought in the show ring are less important in hunting. Bite and teeth alignment are not an issue. A good length of muzzle is nice, but Cockers with shorter muzzles also retrieve well. The luxuriant Cocker coat is a liability in the field, so a shorter haircut is in order. If your Cocker is being shown while getting ready for later field work, much of the training can be done in full coat.

Equipment

For training and hunting, you need collars and leads. Buckle collars are the most common. Wide, bright-orange collars make the dogs more visible and clearly identifies them as working hunting dogs. Some owners put a plate or tag on the collar. Put only your phone number and the word "reward" on the tag. Including your dog's name enables whoever finds the dog to bond with her, whereas the word "reward" encourages her return.

Several leads may be used. The basic is nylon five- to six-feet long. A flexi-lead can be useful in training retrieving. A long line can be used for training if your Cocker is not yet reliable off-lead.

You will need to wear a bright blaze orange vest or jacket in the field. All

Birds for the test.

You cannot use devices to control your dog at a hunt test or field trial. Among the equipment disallowed are prong collars, electronic collars, muzzles, or head collars.

Puppy Training

Hunt training begins almost as soon as you get your Cocker Spaniel.

The first and most important thing you can do is to get to know your Cocker, to develop a bond with her. What is her temperament like? Her personality? Is she playful or serious? Shy or pushy? What excites her—food, toys, balls? Your knowledge of her is critical to how you plan her training, and your relationship will help her see you as her leader.

Basic Obedience

As with other events and competitions, hunting requires a strong basic obedience foundation with your Cocker. You can work on introductory hunt skills at the same time as you work on obedience. She will need a very reliable recall for when you are working off-lead. She should also dependably *sit* and *stay* on command. You must be able to control your dog in the field.

people, even spectators, are required to wear orange. Hunting vests have pockets to carry water bottles and birds.

You Cocker will need to become accustomed to gunfire. A blank .22 pistol will be used for this. If using a gun isn't possible in some training situations, two blocks of wood banged together will approximate the sound.

Cockers need dummies to retrieve, small ones for puppies and larger ones as they grow. You can make these yourself by wrapping five inches of wood about the diameter of a broom handle in cloth. Your Cocker will graduate from practicing with dummies to practicing with birds.

You will need a whistle, which can be conveniently hung on a lanyard around your neck. It is easier to whistle commands than shout them in the field. Plastic will be more comfortable on your lips than cold metal on near-freezing mornings.

> COCKER CLUE
> Standard whistle commands are used to control dogs in the field.
>
> 1 toot: Sit.
> 2 toots: Turn and run in the opposite direction (when searching for birds).
> 3 toots or 1 long toot: Come.

Retrieving a dummy from water. Notice the undocked, natural Cocker tail.

Retrieving

While many Cockers are natural retrievers, some are not. For both, start retrieving training early.

Training for the hunting retrieve is slightly different than the retrieve used in obedience. While obedience uses dumbbells for retrieving, dogs in hunt training use dummies (also called bumpers), which are usually fabric covered.

Play with your puppy first to get her happy before retrieving exercise. Practice only a few retrieves at a time. Always end the game while she is still interested.

When you toss the dummy, hold your puppy as she watches where it falls, as she will mark—see, notice, and remember—where a bird falls. Then send her on the

retrieve with your arm pointing in the direction you want her to go.

When your Cocker is retrieving reliably, hide the dummy. Use your arm to direct her to the hiding spot and tell her to retrieve. This begins training for a blind retrieve, in which your Cocker will be sent

COCKER CLUE

Monkey see, monkey do, and dogs, too. If you or a friend has a dog who is trained in retrieving and working with birds, let your Cocker watch, perhaps from a crate where she can get a good view. Her interest will be piqued by all the fun the other dog is having. She will also learn some of what you want to teach by watching another dog.

to retrieve a bird she didn't see fall. Don't do more than one or two hidden retrieves per session.

When she returns with you with the dummy, don't wrestle it from her or take it when she doesn't want to give it up. Doing so will make her mouth hard, and she will damage the bird. Try some of the earlier suggestions to have her give up her prize (see Chapter 11).

Successful retrieve.

Introduction to Birds

Some breeders introduce puppies to birds by putting a wing in the pen when the dogs are three to four weeks old, so your Cocker may have already experienced birds.

When your Cocker has been retrieving reliably, tie a bird wing on the dummy. Secure it thoroughly with string so that your puppy won't try to carry the dummy by the wing. The dummy-plus-wing can be stored in the freezer when not in use.

If she is initially afraid of a bird or wing, relax, and let her try again. When she is three or four months old, practice with her briefly for three or four days each week. The goal is to develop an intense interest in birds in your Cocker.

Play hide and seek with the dummy-plus-wing. Dangle a wing on the end of a line attached to a pole, and entice your Cocker to chase it. Elicit her interest, and always leave her wanting more.

Introduction to Cover

As you walk with your Cocker, introduce her to cover—brush and brambles where she may search for and find birds. She's not hunting now, just getting familiar. Let her have fun, play, and explore. One of a Cocker's strengths as a hunting companion is her ability to get into dense cover after birds. Explore different hills, fields, and gullies, so she can become comfortable with various locations. Later she'll focus on birds, not the terrain.

Public land may be available to you. Private lands may be used with permission. Be a good guest; lock gates, don't knock down fences or otherwise abuse

COCKER CLUE

Be familiar with the territories you explore with your Cocker to make sure she will be safe. She may rouse venomous snakes and get bitten. Alligators lurk in southern waters and can eat dogs. Coyotes prey on some dogs in some areas.

the privilege, or you will lose it for yourself and others.

Caring for Your Dog in the Field

Before you head for the field with or without other dogs, make sure that your Cocker is in good health, with all vaccinations up to date.

If your Cocker is not destined for the show ring, give her a short haircut. Leave a moderate amount of coat on her legs and underside for protection from the underbrush. Trim her once a month to keep her coat to a useful length. If you are maintaining a longer coat, you will have more work to do.

Inspect her coat after each excursion. Remove bristles, burrs, or any lingering debris. Brush and comb her coat to remove any tangles before they develop into mats. Texture makes a difference. Cottony coats pick up everything, whereas debris combs out of good coats more easily.

Check for cuts and any injuries; medicate and treat. Inspect her feet carefully, including between her toes, both for debris and abrasions.

Based on anecdotes, black coats may be more durable. White and ASCOB coats stain and break more. Many hunters like white on their Cockers, though, for the dogs are more easily seen at a distance. Roans are reported to have the best noses.

Bring water for your dog to drink. She will be running and working hard, and will need periodic drinks. You can take a small, portable drinking bowl for her, or she can drink from the bottle.

Remember to have your girl wear her bright orange collar, including a tag or plate with your phone number.

A technique called "shaking" can excite your puppy's interest in birds. You'll need an accomplice standing several feet from you, with each of you holding a dead bird. Show your puppy one bird, tease her with it, let her smell it. When she goes for it, raise it beyond her reach, and have your partner call her and show her the other bird. Tease her with the second bird, then raise it out of reach, and

Flushing a bird.

COCKER CLUE

Every sport and specialty has its vocabulary. Here is a sample glossary for hunting with your Cocker.

Back: return to handler
Bevy: flock of birds
Birdy: strong bird-hunting instinct
Blind: a place that a hunter uses as cover
Brace: running two dogs; one dog must honor the other (honor means that the second dog arriving at the situation stands behind the first dog, who gets to flush the bird)
Break: failure to stop at a flush, shot, or command
Decoy: mock water bird used to lure birds of a species within gun range
Delivery: giving the retrieved object or game to the handler
Derby: field trial competition for young, inexperienced dogs
Dummy: object used to teach dog to retrieve

Fall: where a bird came down or landed
Fetch: retrieve and return downed game to the hunter
Flush: drive birds from cover
Futurity stakes: competition class for young dogs nominated for the competition before birth
Game: prey or hunted quarry
Hard-mouthed: dog that damages the bird during the retrieve
Heel: walk next to handler
Hup: alternate to the Sit command in the field
Mark: see the place where game fell prior to the retrieve, then hunter sends dog
Quarter: processes of searching for game side to side in a field ahead of the hunter
Soft-mouth: dog that doesn't damage the birds she carries; or a puppy that drops the bird
Trap: retrieve a bird from cover (rather than flushing it)

call her back to the first bird. After a couple of rounds, toss one of the birds. Encourage her to go to it; see if she will pick it up. Encourage her to bring it to you.

Quartering

Quartering is the process where your Cocker searches for birds, going in a fairly wide zigzag pattern in front of you. Half of the quartering process, moving off to the left or right, is called a cast. Start teaching quartering when your Cocker is

reliably retrieving dummies and dead birds.

Train her to quarter by walking her in the zigzag pattern, 30 yards to either side of center, to cover the field. Keep her on lead to start. At each turn to go in the opposite directions, give her a whistle or word command to change direction. Some dogs take to quartering naturally, while others need more practice.

When she has the concept of quartering and when she is casting in one direction, toss a dead bird in the opposite direction, behind her. She can find it when she returns to hunt in the opposite direction.

Have a partner plant birds in cover when neither you or your Cocker watch where they are put. Your assistant will dizzy the bird or tuck its head under its wing; the bird should stay put long enough for your Cocker to find and flush it. Send your dog to quarter and find the birds.

The wind and the moisture at ground level will greatly affect how quickly and easily your Cocker can find the birds. Have her work into the wind initially, so the scent comes to her. Early morning dew makes the scent stronger and easier to find. As she becomes proficient, you can try her with breezes from different directions. Practice also on different terrain with varying amounts of cover.

Marking

When your Cocker "marks," she sees the bird fall after it is shot. Even though they are short, Cockers are quite good at marking where birds fall. From there, she will go or you will send her to retrieve the downed bird.

A blind retrieve is one where you send your Cocker to a specific area to search for a shot bird, even though she didn't see it fall. You don't necessarily know exactly where it is, but you must indicate the direction in which you want her to search.

Water Work

Retrieving work includes recovering birds from lakes or streams.

Not all dogs are initially good swimmers, so introduce water slowly. You can begin when she is quite young by using a plastic child's pool or a very shallow creek. Let her see other dogs enjoying swimming.

Go in with her and make sure the water is warm enough for both of you. A Cocker's coat offers little protection from freezing water. If she is uncomfortable, don't force her, or she may develop a negative association with water. Let her get acclimated at her own pace.

Creeks are great places for your Cocker to learn about water. There should be no or minimal current and firm footing while she is in shallow water. Preferably, the middle will be deep enough for her to start swimming. The benefit to a creek is that you can easily go across and up the other side. Don't worry if her swimming form isn't perfect at first; she'll get the hang of it. Don't stay in too long; remember the principle of always leaving her wanting more.

Make sure your Cocker can do field work first, including retrieving birds,

Retrieving from water.

A wet coat is heavy. This Cocker would have an easier time with water work if her coat were trimmed shorter.

before starting her on water work. When she is comfortable going in and out of water, you might throw a dummy a yard or two from shore for her to retrieve. As she masters short retrieves, you can make them longer. When you switch to retrieving dead birds from water, make the retrieves short again. A short haircut is recommended for Cockers who will be doing water work. The weight of a water-logged long coat may pull the dog down and can result in drowning.

Introduction to Gunfire

Your Cocker needs to become accustomed to gunfire, for the birds that she flushes will be shot. Gunfire is the last thing to introduce when training for the field. Acquaint your Cocker to gunfire when she won't notice, when she is too focused on eating, playing, or chasing something to notice a small pop. Make the introductory sounds fairly low volume. You can use a recording of the sound or emulate a gunshot by banging two blocks of wood together. If she doesn't notice, do it again the next time she is focused on some distraction. Gradually increase the volume. When she does notice, it will be associated with something good or fun.

When your Cocker chases a bird, shoot a .22 blank gun or cap pistol while she is absorbed in the chase. If she is startled, let her chase several more birds before trying again. If she doesn't notice, shoot when she chases again.

Water retrieving begins with short retrieves with dummies.

Take her to a field trial or hunt test. Don't place her close to the shooting until you see that she is not bothered by it. Let her see that other dogs are not upset by the sound. Let her watch other dogs hunt; it will give her the idea of what she will be doing, and get her excited.

One place absolutely not to take her is the local gun range. It is much too loud and may ruin her usefulness as a hunting companion.

Help with Training

In all sports, there are professionals who are paid for their expertise, including those who will train your Cocker to hunt. If you don't have the time or inclination to train your dog, you can send her to a professional.

If you choose to train on your own, work with like-minded people who are also training their spaniels. Help each other with suggestions and possible solutions to problems. You can find such folk at local hunt or field clubs. Some problems, however, can use the input of an expert. Confer with a professional for problems you cannot work out for yourself.

Every method and technique doesn't work equally well on all Cockers. You can get excellent ideas from knowledgeable amateurs as well as professionals.

Useful Addresses, Web Sites, and Literature

Organizations

Agility Association of Canada
638 Wonderland Road South
London, Ontario
N6K 1L8
(519) 473-3410
www.aac.ca

American Kennel Club
8051 Arco Corporate Drive, Suite 100
Raleigh, NC 27617-3390
(919) 233-9767
www.akc.org

American Spaniel Club
P.O. Box 4194
Frankfort, KY 40604
E-mail: ASC.Secretary@gmail.com
www.asc-cockerspaniel.org

Canadian Kennel Club
89 Skyway Avenue
Suite 100
Etobicoke, Ontario
M9W 6R4
(416) 675-5511
www.ckc.ca

North American Dog Agility Council
P.O. Box 1206
Colbert, OK 74733
(208) 689-3803
www.nadac.com

United States Dog Agility Association
P.O. Box 850955
Richardson, TX 75085
(972) 487-2200
www.usdaa.com

Web Sites

Canine Health Foundation
www.akcchf.org

CERF (Canine Eye Registry Foundation)
www.vmdb.org

Cockers in the Field
www.fieldcockers.com

Great Lakes American Cocker Spaniel
 Hunting Enthusiasts
http://userpages.chorus.net/hunsaker/
 Glacshe.Html

North American Flyball Association
www.flyball.org

Orthopedic Foundation for Animals
www.offa.org

Books

Austin, Norman and Jean. *The Complete American Cocker Spaniel*. New York, NY: Howell Book House, 1993.

Coile, D. Caroline. *The Cocker Spaniel Handbook*. Hauppauge, NY: Barron's Educational Series, 2007.

___. *Show Me! A Dog Showing Primer*. Hauppauge, NY: Barron's Educational Series, 1997.

Donaldson, Jean. *Culture Clash*. Berkley, CA: James Kenneth Publishers, 1997.

Grandin, Temple and Catherine Johnson. *Animals in Translation*. Orlando, FL: Harcourt, Inc., 2005.

McConnell, Patricia. *The Other End of the Leash*. New York, NY: Ballantine Books, 2002.

Pryor, Karen. *Don't Shoot the Dog!* New York, NY: Bantam Books, 1999.

___. *Getting Started: Clicker Training for Dogs*. Waltham, MA: Sunshine Books Inc., 1999.

Roettger, Anthony Z. and Benjamin H. Schleider III. *Urban Gun Dogs: Training*

Flushing Dogs for Home & Field. Cranston, RI: The Writers' Collective, 2005.

Spencer, James B. *HUP! Training Flushing Spaniels The American Way*. Loveland, CO: Alpine Publications, 2002.

Periodicals

AKC Gazette
www.akc.org
Contact AKC for subscription information.

The American Cocker Magazine
14531 Jefferson Street
Department CP
Midway City, CA 92655
www.cyberpet.com/cyberdog/products/ pubmag/premier.html

The Cocker Classic
912 Hemlock Road
Carson, WA 98610
www.cockerclassic.com

Spaniels in the Field
5312 Wolf Knoll Road
Orr, MN 55771
www.spanielsinthefield.com

Index

A-Frame, 109, 110, 112
Aggression, 35, 86, 87
Agility, 6, 9, 16, 80, 108–115
Agility
    Maturity, 109
    Obstacles, 108–110, 114,
    115
    Titles, 110, 112, 114
American Kennel Club/AKC,
    3, 4, 11, 13, 14, 23,
    106, 119, 120, 130
Allergies, 58
American Spaniel Club/ASC,
    3, 12, 13, 106, 130
Attention, 32, 33, 37, 87, 91
Attitude, 10
Autoimmune disorders, 59
Avoidance, 25
Avoidance, problem, 81

Baby gate, 20, 27, 28
Baiting, 101, 103
Barking, 84
Bathing, 70, 71, 73
Bed, 18, 21, 27
Belly band, 83
Birds, 22, 122, 124–128
Birds, 122
Body language, 38
Body language, dog, 45, 46
Bones, 18, 68, 81, 84, 90
Books, 133
Boundaries, 27
Breeder
    Backyard, 10, 14
    Commercial, 10, 14
    Companion event, 9

Hunting, 10
    Reputable, 10–13
    Responsible, 8, 15, 24
    Show, 8–9
Broad jump, 111
Brushes, 66
Brushing, 31, 67, 69–71, 104,
    125

Canine Good Citizen (CGC),
    53, 80, 91, 92
Car travel, 30, 31
Cataracts, 57
CERF Canine Eye Registration
    Foundation, 57
Championship, 6, 7, 100
Cherry eye, 56
Chewing, 84, 85
Children, 4, 21, 44, 53, 54
Clicker, 44, 45, 80
Clipper, care, 72
Clippers, 66, 72, 73
Clothes, dog, 19
Coat, 1, 121, 125, 128
Coat, care, 69–73, 104
Coat, grooming, 31, 69–73
Coat, trimming, 71–73
Collar, 16, 30, 74, 90, 101,
    116, 121, 122, 125
Collar
    Bark, 84
    Buckle, 16
    Flea, 61
    Martingale, 16, 30, 101
    Orange, 121, 125
    Quick-clip, 16
    Rolled leather, 16

Show, 30, 101
Slip, 16, 101
Color, 5, 125
Color
    ASCOB, 5, 6
    Black, 5
    Parti, 5
    Roan, 5
    Tan points, 5
Come, 76, 77
Command, give once, 43
Communication, 36
Communication, tone of
    voice, 37
Communication, words, 37
Companion Dog, 94, 95
Companion Dog Excellent, 95
Conformation, 100
    gait, 102
    handling, 105
    training, 101
Contact zones, 109, 110,
    112, 113
Contract, sales, 13
Correction, 39, 41, 42, 82, 83
Cover, 124
Crate, 19, 21, 27, 30
Crate, training, 27

Debarking, 84
Dental care, 68
Description, 1
Diarrhea, 62
Digging, 86
Distractions, 43, 44, 77
Dodge, Mrs. Geraldine
    Rockefeller, 3

Dog clubs, 12, 103, 106
Dog show, purpose, 14, 100
Dog walk, 113
Dog-proof, home, 20
Down, 76
Down, long, 95
Drop on recall, 95
Dry eye, 56
Dummies, 122–124, 126

Ear, care, 67, 68
Ears, 20, 28, 29, 46, 49, 55, 56, 58, 67, 68, 70, 72, 98
Ectropion, 56
English Cocker Spaniel, 3, 4
Entropion, 56
Epilepsy, 60
Exercise, 63, 64, 82, 89, 104
Exercise pen, 20, 27
Eyes, 56

Fence, 21, 27
Field trials, 120
Finish, 92, 93
Flea collar, in vacuum cleaner, 61
Flea comb, 66
Flyball
  ball box, 116, 118
  balls, 116
  height dog, 116
  organizations, 116
  points, 116
  teams, 118
  training, 117
Food, canned, 28
Food, dog, 14, 20, 28
Food, kibble, 28
Food, moist, 28
Free feeding, 28

Garbage, 89
Gender, 6
Glaucoma, 57
Glossary, hunting, 126
Groomers, 65
Groomers, selecting, 65
Grooming supplies, 19
Grooming table, 66
Grooming, equipment, 66
Grooming, session, 31
Grooming, training, 31, 66, 67
Guns, 122, 128, 129

Hand signal, 37, 38, 75, 76, 120
Handling, 24, 31, 51, 104, 105
Health checklist, 63
Health record, 13, 14, 22
Heartworm, 60, 61
Heel, 77, 78
Hip dysplasia, 58
History, 1–4
Housetraining, 25–27, 82
Hunt test, 6, 119–121
Hunt test, titles, 119, 121
Hunt tests, AKC, 119, 120
Hyperactivity, 89

Jump, broad, 96
Jump, high, 96
Jumping, 85–86
Jumps, 96, 97, 110, 111

Lead
  Flexible, 17
  Long line, 17
  Show, 30, 101
  Training, 30
Leader, 38

Leader, of the pack, 46–48
Leader, posture, 38, 39
Leads, 16, 17, 30, 74, 90, 101, 121
Leave it, 33
Life span, 7
Liver recipe, 40

Mange, 61, 62
Mark, 123, 126, 127
Massage, 31
Matches, 103
Mats, 16, 57, 61, 66, 69–71, 125
Microchip, 16, 22
Mites, 61, 62
Mites, ear, 55
Mouth, soft, 2, 10, 120
Mouthing, 88, 89

Nail, trimming, 66, 68, 69
Name, 23
Noise, 50–52

Obedience, 6, 9, 74, 80
  classes, 16, 79, 80, 91
  clubs, 79, 97, 108
  trainers, 79
Obo, 3
OFA, 59, 133
Organizations, 130

Parasites, 61
Patellar luxation, 58, 59
Patience, 33
Pause table, 110
Pedigree, 13
People, meeting, 51
Periodicals, 133
Pet quality, 10
Pets, other, 21

PFK Phosphofructokinase
    deficiency, 59, 60
Plants, poisonous, 20
Playpen, puppy, 26
Popularity, 4, 10, 11
Predators, 125
Professional handler, 105
Professional trainer, 79, 129
Progressive retinal atrophy
    (PRA), 57
Proofing, 93
Puppy kindergarten, 16
Puppy mill, 10
Puppy or Adult, 14, 15

Quartering, 126

Rally, 92
    advanced, 93
    excellent, 93
    honor exercise, 93
    levels, 93
    novice, 93
    stations, 93, 94
    titles, 94
Red Brucie, 3
Registration, certificate, 14
Registration, full, 14
Registration, limited, 14
Reinforcement,
    intermittent, 41
Release, 33
Rescue, 15
Resource guarding, 87, 88
Retrieve, 95, 96, 123, 124
Retrieve, water, 127
Rewards, 39–41, 74, 85
Running away, 90

Schedule, 22, 25, 26, 28
Seborrhea, 55, 58

Separation anxiety, 89
Shaping behavior, 40, 41
Show, attitude, 104, 105
Show conditioning, 104
Shyness, 88
Sit, 74–76
    automatic, 78
    long, 95
Size, 1
Skeletal problems, 58, 59
Skin problems, 57, 58
Smells, 52
Snood, 19, 20, 28, 29
Socialization, 49–52
Spaniels, land, 2, 3
Spay, neuter, 64
Stacking, 101, 102
Stages, of life, 36
Stages, of puppy
    development, 50
Standard, excerpts, 101
Stay, 78, 79, 92
Stud dog, 7
Styptic powder, 66, 69
Submissive urination, 83
Superintendents, dog
    show, 12
Supervision, 21, 25, 84, 86
Swimming pool, 5

Table scraps, 28
Tail
    docking, 1, 9
    undocked, 123
Teeter, 113, 114
Temperament, 4, 5, 7, 11,
    24, 34, 35, 48, 49, 54,
    104
Therapy dogs, 53, 54
Therapy dogs,
    organizations, 54

Three-second rule, 42
Timing, 42, 43
Tire jump, 111
Touch, 39
Toys, 17, 18, 47
Track, laying, 99
Tracking
    Equipment, 98
    Tests, 98
    Titles, 98
    Training, 99
Training
    Classes, 52
    Clicker, 44, 45
    Session, 43
Treats, 29, 40, 46, 47, 51, 74,
    75, 77, 87, 90
    earned, 29
Tunnel, closed, 112, 113
Tunnel, open, 112

Utility, 97

Vaccines, 60
Varieties, 3, 5, 100
Vest, hunting, 121, 122
Veterinarian, 22, 55–63
Veterinarian, choosing,
    62
Vinegar, white, 26

Wait, 92
Watching another dog, 43,
    52, 108, 115, 118, 123
Water, 29
Water, swimming, 127, 128
Weave poles, 113, 114
Web sites, 130, 133
Weight, 1, 29
Whistle commands, 122
Worms, intestinal, 62